Stop the Lecturing: Start the Conversation!

Increasing your children's Emotional
Intelligence

Susan Harris Sidsworth BA, MA RCC

Table of Contents

Forward

The Socratic Method of dialogue is a method of communication that stimulates debates, inquires and discussions from individuals who potentially have opposing viewpoints. This book will discuss how parents can use this type of dialogue to develop emotional intelligence in their children. Emotional Intelligence was first described by two Yale university psychologists in the 1990's – Peter Salove and John Mayer, These psychologists identified five areas of EQ or Emotional Intelligence

1. Self awareness

2. Handling emotions appropriately

3. Self motivation (impulse control and delayed self gratification)

4. Empathy

5. Social skills related to handling the emotions in relationships and conflict resolution.

As Parents we often want our children to posses these qualities; however, the focus of parenting always seems to be on intellectual activities or physical activities with the hope that their children will develop these five skills naturally. These skills do not come

naturally for most children. Therefore, this book explores a type of dialogue for parents to use with their children in all different age groups that will help develop these five areas of emotional intelligence.

Often as parents we find ourselves having different and opposing ideas than our children and we feel frustrated when we are trying to speak to them. This book will discuss a type of communication strategy that parents can use with children of any age to help spark up conversations as opposed to lectures. This communication style will help decrease arguments and tension. Most importantly this book will help parents speak and communicate with their children in a way that will increase the child's emotional intelligence. Society often focuses on increasing children's IQ (intellectual intelligence) as opposed to EI (emotional intelligence.) The Socratic Method of Dialogue is a tool parents can use at any time during the day to help stimulate their children to become critical thinkers and understand their emotional responses. By having a greater understanding of their emotional responses children, pre-teens and teens will increase their emotional intelligence

Chapter 1

What is the Socratic Method of Dialogue?

Establishing a dialogue with our children is crucial for our children's emotional and social growth. When we establish dialogue or two –way communications with our children we are become a part of their learning equation. We have many lessons to teach our children, but our children also have many lessons to teach us. Unfortunately, many of us are trapped in a monologue style of communication. We are telling our children what they can and can not do, we are explaining the rules, we are setting boundaries and we are often not listening to our children. Perhaps you want to protest at this point and say that you do listen to your children and that you try to patiently answer all of their questions. And children are generally asking many questions of the journalistic interrogation kind – Why? Where? When How? What? The fact that children are asking these questions is an indication of their quest to understand the world and the demands that it is making on them. But simply answering a child's questions – patiently or impatiently – is not a true dialogue. A dialogue occurs when two or more people engage in conversation about a subject or a decision and take turns asking questions and listening to responses. The ideal Socratic Method involves the asking and answering of questions in order to stimulate critical thinking. The opposite of dialogue is a monologue. One person is speaking and others are supposed to be listening. Since monologues eventually become boring and non-engaging children eventually tune out their parents' monologues. Many parents will finally exclaim in frustration "Am I talking to myself?" and resort to shouting or talking in an angry tone of voice to get their children's attention. Dialogue, on the other hand, is an engagement and an exchange between two people. Parents explain, set rules, dictate behaviours and there is little or no input from children. Since there is reciprocity to dialogue the relationship is more egalitarian and democratic. Children who participate in an autocratic family have less self efficacy – or less belief that they will be heard and that their opinions are important and that they can make choices for themselves that reflect their values and passions. We must begin early employing the Socratic Method with our children so that they learn this pattern of dialogue, exchange, and considered debate and decision making. Engaging in dialogue with our children and assuming that they have opinions and ideas worth listening to right from the beginnings of language formation lays the ground work for positive communication with toddlers, pre-teens, teenagers, and young adults. Since we are adults we know more than our children and it is tempting to "tell" them rather than to engage in Socratic questioning to help them discover information and ideas for themselves. Consider for example a trip to the grocery store. A parent shopping with a young child might tell the child to put some fruit and vegetables into the basket and instruct the child on how to pick apples or bananas that are ripe or vegetables that are fresh. Then the parent can help the child to pick the fruits and vegetables and put them into the grocery cart. The child has learned something valuable about how to select fruits and vegetables, and after repeated lessons the child can then perform the task for him/herself. Certainly this is a positive parenting scenario particularly if the parent is patient and takes the extra time to explain how fruits and vegetables are selected. Consider how this learning situation might be changed if a parent employed Socratic questioning so that children could deduce answers for themselves rather than having them given to them. Socratic questioning begins by asking the children a question to see what they know. On the way to the grocery store the parent might ask "How can we pick the best fruit and vegetables? Does anybody know?" If children are very young they may need some more information. The parent might say we gather information about the world through our senses – sight, sound, smell, touch - Which of these senses do you think might help us to pick the best vegetables when we are in the grocery store?" Engaging in dialogue and Socratic questioning with children on the way to perform the chore keeps them focused on the task being performed and they do not get the feeling that they are baggage you need to haul along with you while you get your chores done. Once you are in the grocery store the Socratic questioning can continue. Send the children to pick out bananas and ask them what colors they will look for and how the fruit might smell or feel to the touch. Asking the questions rather than telling the children what color the fruit should be or how it should feel engages them in a critical thought process.

When we establish a dialogue with our children we get to know them as individuals, and when we consciously remind ourselves to ask children questions about their thoughts, their dreams, their ideas, and their preferences we are also helping children to know and understand themselves. So the benefit to employing the Socratic Method is as follows:

1: Children develop a sense of self awareness and they begin to think about whom they are and how they define themselves in the world and in their family.

2. Parents are able to stop lecturing and help children come to their own logical conclusions and judgments.

Employing the Socratic Method also helps parents stop imposing their own interpretations of their children by labelling or interpreting the child... How many times have you heard a parent say "Oh he/she is just shy, that's why he/she is not answering your questions?" Or many parents will tell the child "You are angry right now and I am not going to talk to you until you stop being angry." In this case the parent has both labelled the child and told the child how he/she feels and used coercion (refusal to speak to the child) to get the child to stop displaying what the parent perceives as unacceptable behaviours. It is far better to begin by asking the children questions about how they are feeling. Questions enable the child to think about the situation and try to identify their own emotions rather than having those emotions identified for them. So in this case a parent might ask the child "Do you think you are feeling angry or disappointed right now, or is there another word you can think of to describe how your are feeling right now?" If the child is having an angry outburst or a tantrum in a public space or at home then the parents or caretakers can let the child know that the behaviour is unacceptable, and then pose the question. Stating in a calm voice that the child's behaviour is an unacceptable way to express emotion , and then posing the question about the child's feelings may be enough to reactivate the child's ability to control him/herself and may act as a catalyst to get the child think about his/her actions. Sometimes with younger children humour works well to help them understand standards of appropriateness. The parent might ask "If I was upset do you think it would be "ok" for me to run around the store and yell at everyone and knock cans off the shelves?" The Socratic

Method of dialogue will help children in recognizing their

emotions and the strategies they employ to deal with and express

their emotions. The basic strategy of Socratic questioning works

well to enhance our communications with children no matter what

age they are. However, the way we pose questions and the

additional resources we bring to the task of parenting need to be

age appropriate.

Employing the Socratic Method gives the parent insight into

their children's comprehension level and into their pattern of

reasoning. Parents want to empower their children to think

logically for themselves in order to produce a good outcome.

Parents often inadvertently undermine their children's ability to

reason or think out a solution by imposing rules and regulations

without explanations and by having a set solution or protocol in

mind. We should encourage children to think about the different

strategies or behaviours we could employ in order to get the

desired outcome. There is generally more than one strategy to

resolve a problem, but parents are often focused on their own

solutions. For example, parents might impose rules about morning routines and the order in which tasks are accomplished such as getting up and getting dressed for school, making beds, readying school supplies and eating breakfast. If the desired outcome is that children should be ready to leave the house for school at a specific time in the morning, then parents should allow children to brainstorm about the best possible way to achieve this goal and allow them to experiment with various strategies in order to come up with the best possible plan for themselves. A child might choose to sleep in his school clothing in order to save time dressing in the mourning. However, this strategy might not work so well if a child has to put on a freshly pressed school uniform. But parents need to be open minded about unusual solutions to problems!

Of course the older children get the more complex the problems and issues are that they need to address. And the older they get the more important it become for them to develop their own reasoning abilities. Parents and caretakers or authority figures will not always be available to oversee decision making and veto poor judgements. It is particularly important for preteens to develop and strengthen their logical reasoning skills so that they will be prepared to handle the greater freedoms and the increased peer pressure that they will experience during their teen years. Unfortunately, helicopter parenting has become the norm in the last fifteen years and children are over supervised and over protected. Parents need to allow children the freedom to take on responsibility for decision making in as many areas of their lives as possible rather than constantly intervening and solving problems for children or explicitly providing solutions for them. For example, if children lose track of homework assignments and fail to hand them in on time, helicopter parents will intervene and provide a note to the teacher so that their children do not have to face the consequences of poor decision making. Or parents will sit down with children and "help" them complete homework to the extent that their children are not taking responsibility for examining the homework assignment and devising a logical plan for completing that assignment on time. When preteens are learning these lessons about reasoned solutions to problems, the stakes are low. If they get a poor grade on a homework assignment in grade six or if they have to miss a sporting event or a game or practice because they have to stay late at school and complete work, there are minimal implications for their future prospects. If young people are still learning these lessons about time management and project management when they are attending college or university, the consequences are definitely more far reaching.

This is not to say that parents should remove themselves from the equation completely. Of course it is important for parents to provide guidance and a sense of direction no matter what the age of the child. In situations like these if parents employ the technique of Socratic Questioning they will be issuing an unspoken invitation to the child to behave in a more adult or mature fashion and take responsibility for him/herself. It is important for parents to remember that part of the solution should always be to engage their children in dialogue. Remember the old saying that if you are not part of the solution, then you are part of the problem. This saying applies to our children as well. Sometimes, however, as parents we struggle to ensure that our children are part of the solution and are actively engaged in finding the solution that works best for them. If we think back upon the example of children getting ready for school on time we can consider the difference between Rigid parenting and the parent who uses Socratic Dialoguing to make children part of the solution process. The more rigid parent might say "Here is a timeline chart of the morning routine. I expect you to get up when the alarm goes off and take fifteen minutes to dress and make your bed. Breakfast is at eight sharp and then everyone must be washed up and have their school bags packed and be ready to leave the house at eight thirty." A parent using Socratic Dialogue can engage the child or children in the planning process. Initiate the dialogue by having everyone gather at a family meeting and describing the problem and asking them to brainstorm for solutions. "We are having difficulty making it out of the house in the morning and it is important that we are on time for school and work. Can anyone think of any solutions to this problem?" As children propose their solutions ask or pose more questions about the particular solution so that more problem solving thought processes are engaged in. If a child proposes sleeping in his school clothes to save his time dressing in the morning do not laugh off this suggestion. The parent might say "Can you foresee any potential problems with this solution?" And if the problem is wrinkled clothing then the child would see that the solution might not be the most suitable. Sometimes parents are too quick to dismiss creative or unusual solutions to problems. We want to encourage creative problem solving in children so we should not be too quick to dismiss their ideas even if from an adult perspective these solutions seem unworkable or odd.

Now that readers have a basic understanding of the Socratic Method, we need to delve into how this method can be applied in age appropriate ways and in various circumstances. The rest of the book will focus on different developmental areas and provide information to parents on how to stimulate children's development of their emotional intelligence by using the Socratic Method to stimulate critical thinking while they are growing into adulthood. The three areas that I would like to address are emotional growth, social growth, and intellectual growth. When I ask parents about their aspirations for their children they will usually indicate that they want their children to have strong self esteem and that they want their children to have a strong sense of who they are as people – that is they hope that their children will have faith that they are people who can achieve the goals they set for themselves and that their children will be able to develop passions and interests and that they will feel positive about their abilities to excel and achieve in the areas that they have chosen for themselves. Other parenting books provide explicit advice on how to use praise and encouragement to foster children's resiliency and their self esteem. Parenting books will also encourage parents to show respect for their children's individuality and instruct them to try and discover their children's talents and innate abilities by exposing them to various experiences and opportunities. And one cannot argue with this essentially good advice. However, many parents report that despite following the advice offered by parenting gurus, they are still having difficulty understanding their children and fostering a strong sense of confidence. Employing the Socratic Method will give all parents the tools they need to truly understand their children and employing this method will also make empowerment and self-esteem a part of the child's daily routine. Many parents may feel that employing this type of Socratic dialogue is too time consuming and they may feel that the exchange is unnatural or that they have to put too much effort into daily tasks and rituals. However, the more we engage in Socratic dialogues with our children the more these dialogues become a habitual part of our interaction and routines. This is not to say that every interaction and exchange must be based upon the Socratic Method. It is perfectly acceptable to recognize when it is necessary to employ more rigid, rule bound interactions with our children. However, parents if children must, for the majority of the time, listen to your commands and requests and comply or be punished, then they are bound to feel like they can have little influence over the conditions and outcomes of their lives.

Chapter Two:

How to Establish Emotional Intelligence in Babies and Toddlers

Parents might think that it is impossible to use Socratic Dialogue with children who are not yet verbal. But even before children become verbal and have the ability to express themselves by using words, they are communicating their emotions to us. Parents can begin to establish the pattern of Socratic Dialogue with their children even before their children begin to speak. Many parents will do this instinctively because they have an innate recognition that communication needs to be a two way street, so they will begin to engage in "conversation" with their babies even before the babies can speak. For example if the baby is crying and needs a diaper change, the communicative parent will pick up the baby and talk to the baby rather than simply picking up the baby and performing the "chore" of changing the diaper. The parent who is laying the ground work for Socratic Dialogue speaks directly to the baby and puts words to the emotions that the baby is expressing.

"You're telling me that you need a diaper change, aren't you? Well let's get you into a nice dry diaper so that you'll feel better." Babies who are addressed directly when they send out a communication signal learn quickly about expressing their emotions and their needs, and that the message they have sent has been received. Parents who want to raise children who are good communicators will respond to their baby's signals and name the emotion that the baby is expressing. "There. I can tell by that smile that you are feeling much better. Do you want to play now? I think you are telling me that you want to play now." Usually parents will instinctively match the tone of their voice to the emotion that the baby is expressing by using a sadder, lower tone to comment on the baby's distress and using a brighter, happier tone to express the baby's joy or contentment. Using appropriate tones and words and speaking the messages that the baby is sending to you through nonverbal cues establishes the pattern and the idea of dialogue. Researchers have found that babies cross culturally respond to infant-directed speech. That is babies recognize when speech is directed towards them rather than when speech is just part of the background noise. And there is evidence of increased blood flow to the baby's frontal lobes when the baby is exposed to infant directed speech. So the evidence shows that it is important to direct speech towards the baby and to use language and speak to the baby as one would speak to an adult. The difference is, of course, that when parents and caretakers are speaking to babies or infants they use higher pitched voices and they vary the tone of their voice to attract and maintain the baby's attention more so than with adults.

Even very young babies can understand the pattern of dialogue that is being established. When parents look at the child and make eye contact and ask the child a question and then pause, the infant will make a noise in response. Of course when parents respond with positive energy in the terms of facial expression and tone of voice, then the baby is rewarded for engaging in "conversation" and will make further efforts to establish patterns of conversation with parents. Researchers have shown that infants can begin to distinguish the tone of approval or disapproval in parents' voices even when they are four or five months old. The tone of voice conveys the emotion to the child. Children who are exposed to this type of communication learn language more quickly and they seem to be more aware of emotions and better able to communicate their emotions to caretakers and adults. Parents who establish this pattern of Socratic dialogue with their children when they are still infants enhance the chances of their children having a higher EQ or emotional intelligence. Every cultural group varies in the amount of emotion or expressiveness that is part of communication, but in all cultures parents and caretakers will be more emotionally expressive when speaking with infants. We exaggerate the emotion in order to help children determine the emotion being expressed. Exaggerated tones of voice are often accompanied by exaggerated facial expressions. Putting words to the emotions of young children before they themselves have the words to express their emotions prepares them for later expressing their emotions verbally.

One strategy for engaging pre-verbal children in a Socratic pattern of exchange and helping them to learn the skill of emotional expression is to use a felt board or a picture book with various facial expressions on character's faces. Have the child point to a particular picture on the board or in the book and ask the question "Is the boy happy?" Then the parent can mimic the expression and ask the question again "Is Daddy/Mummy happy?" Children will quickly learn to identify the emotion that is being acted out by the parent or the emotion displayed by the character in the picture. A picture book like **Glad Monster, Sad Monster** by Ed Emberly is a good example of a book that can be shared even with children who cannot yet speak. Another strategy is to take pictures of your child's face or your face with different expressions and then make them in to flashcards and show them to the baby while naming the emotion. It is important to use the question and answer pattern when doing this so that the child can step into the role of supplying the answer. "Do you think the baby is sad or happy?" Then the parent pauses and provides the answer. "The baby is happy." These types of activities lay the ground work for strengthening your child's ability to recognize his/her own emotions and the emotions of others, and these exercises also lay the ground work for communication and the expression of emotions through the use of words.

Picture books and singing songs or posing questions and helping to provide answers works well with preverbal children usually under the age of two. Children between the ages of two and five can engage in more dramatic play and interactions that strength the groundwork that you have laid down with the younger child.

Reading picture books is a good place to begin with 3-5 year olds as well. For example, **Franklin's Bad Day** by Paulette Bougoise helps children to explore the angry and upset feeling they might experience when a friend moves away. Once you have read the book to children it is important to engage in Socratic Dialogue. You want the children to really think about the characters and why they experienced the emotions they did and what choices they made about how to express those emotions. It is always less threatening for children to talk about the characters in a book than to talk about themselves or their friends. So it is better to begin the dialogue by asking questions about the characters in the story and then by asking children if they can think of a time when they felt like the character in the story. Sometimes it is helpful for children to act out the characters in the story since this type of imaginative activity also gives children an insight into their emotions and a felling of some control over their emotions. For example after reading children the story about Franklin the parent might ask the question "Do you think Franklin was mean because he was feeling angry?" After children have discussed the story character parents can ask "Has someone ever been mean to you because they were angry? Or have you ever been mean to someone else because you were angry?" Engaging in these types of Socratic Dialogues gives parents an opportunity to get to know their children as well. Parents might ask "What are some of the things that make you angry?" Parents are often surprised by the answers that their children give and they may not have been aware of some of the actions that they have taken that have angered their children. Remember that the purpose of engaging in Socratic Dialogue is to learn to appreciate another person's pint of view. All too often parents are focused on their own point of view and are more concerned with imposing their values or rules. It is important for parents to explore some of the feelings their children may have about the rules and regulations or even their conflicts and interactions with parents. Of course, this is a two- way Street since children are also often not aware of their parents' feelings and they can be so wrapped up in processing their own emotions that they may not consciously identify that their parents can be angry or upset or frustrated. The more parents and children can get into the habit of identifying their emotions with words and engage in exploratory dialogues about the source of these emotions –positive and negative – and the best way to deal with them and express them – the better chance children have of developing a higher EQ or emotional intelligence.

Chapter Three

How to Establish Emotional Intelligence in School Aged Children

Once children go to school and begin to participate in peer groups they are faced with greater challenges in terms of dealing with negative and positive emotions and learning appropriate ways to express those emotions. Appropriate parent role modeling is the best way to help children develop their communication skills and their capacity to understand their own and other people's emotions. First think about how affection and positivity are expressed in your household to your children. Do you give warm and affectionate hugs to your children? Do you express your approval and love by offering praise and encouragement? Children who receive this kind of emotional support from their parents will mimic these positive behaviours in their interactions with friends and peers. It is helpful to have discussions with children about what are the appropriate ways to express affection to family members and to peers, teachers, and family friends and other adults. Children should also be given an opportunity to express their preferences for how they like to express affection and how they like others to express affection towards them. It is important to consider whether or not traditional gender roles are impacting the way expressions of affection are conveyed within the family. Families that focus on traditional masculine and feminine roles may inadvertently fail to nourish the emotional intelligence of boys in the family since they may require boys to be less emotionally expressive and less in need of affection and warmth. However, parents should not assume that all children are the same in terms of how much physical affection and how much verbal affection they prefer. Having a Socratic Dialogue about likes and dislikes in regards to the way people express affection can provide both parents and children with insights into personal preferences and comfort zones. If Grandma or another relative "smothers" a child with hugs or physical affection – then the child has a right to say that he/she prefers not to be hugged not so tightly. It is important for children to feel like they have control over the way they express physical affection and that they have a right to tell people about their preferences and set boundaries with others. Listen to your children and show respect for their opinions and they will learn how to manage their emotions and show respect for others. Openly showing affection and openly discussing emotions helps children to develop a sense of empathy for others.

A more difficult task for all of us– children included – is what to do with our negative emotions and how to express them. Do not dismiss children feelings by patronizing them or down playing the situation and telling them they are foolish to be afraid or angry. These types of statements just cause children to develop a mistrust of their own emotional responses. It is far better to explore these negative emotions through Socratic Dialogue. It is, however, acceptable to intervene and tell the child who is hitting or lashing out at others or shouting that this type of behaviour is unacceptable. But remember there is a difference between telling the child that the **behaviour** is unacceptable and the **emotion** is unacceptable. Be sure you are making this distinction clear to your child. Many parents are tempted to respond to the situation by saying: "Your behaviour is ridiculous. You have no reason to be angry". However, responses such as these will not help children to have a higher Emotional Intelligence and such responses will not help them to understand their own emotions and evaluate their appropriateness. If children are too upset to think about their emotional responses then they made need some de-stressing time or some quiet time so that they can get their emotions under control, and when they are calmer the parents can engage in Socratic Dialogue to help them arrive at an understanding of their response and an evaluation of whether or not this was the best way to express their emotions. The effort to help your children be introspective or self reflective and better understand their emotional responses is well worth it. Studies have shown that Emotional Intelligence is a strong predictor of future career success and future success in forming relationships with peer and partners. Socratic Dialogue helps children to be introspective and self reflective. Being able to understand one's emotional responses is a necessary step on the path to emotional self control and emotional self regulation.

For example, if you are out shopping with your school aged child and he/she asks you to purchase a new video game and you refuse, the child may respond by being rude or shouting and getting angry. In this case you can begin to engage in dialogue with the child, but remember to focus on the important issue which is the child's behaviour, and not his/her request for the video game. Many parents may make the mistake of engaging in questions about why the child wants the video game; however, if the child is using sulking, shouting or other negative behaviours to sway the parents' decision making then he/she is engaging in a form of emotional bullying. If we want our children to grow up to be respectful adults who listen to others and discuss issues in a way that is solution focused and that takes into account every one's opinions, then we need to make sure we role model this behaviour. We do our children no favours when we give in to negative behaviours such as these because positive reinforcement means that children will use the strategy of emotional bullying when ever they want their opinions or their choices to prevail. You can try and bring the child around to the proper behaviours by making an observation and posing a question. Making an observation or a statement is the parents' opportunity to teach children about their values and expectations. The parent in this situation might say: "I can see you are upset because we cannot purchase the video game now. Can you think of a better strategy for handling your disappointment? And would you like to discuss the possibility of purchasing this video game while we are making dinner tonight? Be sure to pause and give your children time to think and respond. Sometimes parents in this situation will launch into a lecture mode because they become upset and angry themselves when their children are being rude in public since they feel that such behaviours reflect badly upon them. And sometimes children genuinely seem unable to be called back from the brink; that is they are unable to control their emotions and they are determined to be rude and angry and obnoxious. If children are not rational and are over whelmed by the emotions they are experiencing, then there is no point in engaging in any kind of Socratic Dialogue. In the scenario painted above the two questions posed may give the child pause for thought and he/she may be able to recognize their disappointment and anger and respond to these questions. However, if the child can not be nudged in the direction of greater self control then it is important for parents to change the situation immediately. Take the child away from the situation immediately and give him/her some time to pause and reflect on the behaviour.

Between the ages of six and 12 children will develop in leaps and bounds in terms of their intellectual, social, and emotional growth. While all of these aspects of growth are linked, often parents will **not** focus on activities that strengthen children's Emotional Intelligence; instead, parents will focus energy and resources on intellectual pursuits that they feel will strengthen children's skills, work habits, and intellectual abilities. Children will often be exposed to extra curricular activities that focus on physical fitness or enhancement of intellectual skills such as math, vocabulary or language. However, the emotional side of the equation is often dealt with in a haphazard fashion. Parents need to put some conscious thought into creative activities that they can engage in with children to help them explore and understand emotions. The ideal age to engage in these activities is between the ages of 6-9. As children progress through the lower grades of elementary school to the upper grades – grades five through seven- they begin to focus more on activities with peer groups and are less involved in creative play with parents. Therefore, parents need to make optimal use of these years to find teachable moments so that children will enter these upper elementary grades with a strong

Emotional Intelligence so that they have high self esteem and are better equipped to deal with peer pressures and the intricacies of social interactions in same and opposite sex peer groups. Engaging in creative play and creative activities that helps your children to better understand their own feelings and the feelings of others and prepares them for forming friendships and fostering those friendships as they go through their elementary school years. Children with a sense of empathy – the ability to appreciate and understand another person's point of view and that person's feelings – are more likely to form friendships with peers. The ability to form friendships is crucial for children as they become independent of parents and rely more on their own initiative for arranging social activities with playmates. Exclusion from friendship groups and struggles with maintaining friendships are detrimental to children's overall development. As they progress through their elementary school years a failure to forge friendship bonds and a friendship circle can have a significant impact on children's self esteem and sense of self respect. Children who form friendships at school are less lonely, less likely to report feelings of sadness and more likely to report liking school. By making and managing friendships during these elementary school years children are laying the groundwork for the emotional skills that they will need to negotiate friendships and romantic relationships during their teen years.

Dramatic play with children is a good way to initiate Socratic Dialogue with your children that will enable them to explore emotions that they will experience as they enter and exit friendship circles during their elementary school years. Story telling, creative movement, short dramatic skits – these are all ways of initiating conversation and increasing children's confidence about expressing and recognizing emotions. Think of common situations that children might need to deal with as they venture out in the world and help them to prepare for these situations by using creative activities at home. For example children who try to form friendships with others will inevitably feel the sting of rejection when they try to establish a friendship with someone who rebuffs them. A good place to begin exploring this situation is by reading a book or a scene out of a book that deals with the situation. Try and chose a book that is age appropriate. For example, **Charlotte's**

Web by E.B. White features a scene in which Wilbur is lonely and bored and he decides to seek out a friend. He is rebuffed many times and is feeling quite despairing when he hears the voice of Charlotte. Read the scene to children and then initiate a Socratic Dialogue to help them think about the situation. For example, "How do you think Wilbur felt when the other animals would not be his friend?" "Do you think Wilbur felt like giving up on the search for a friend?" "Can you think of a time when you are somebody else you knew felt like Wilbur?" When you read stories to six and seven year olds this will provide them with an opportunity to talk about their own feelings and experiences. Parents are often surprised when they engage in these creative activities to find out that their children are experiencing worries or fears that were not aware of. Ask the librarian at your local library for a list of suitable books that deal with the subject of making friends.

For eight, nine and ten year olds presenting real life scenarios for them to ponder about or act out is a good way to explore the emotions that children will experience as they venture forth and form their friendship circle. For example, "There was a girl in grade three who had lots of friends and she played with them at recess and had her lunch with them. But one day they all were mean to her. Nobody would talk to her or play with her, and her girlfriends were spreading rumours about her." The children can be asked to act out the scenario and then you can engage your children in some Socratic Dialogue, or you can just ask your children questions about the scenario. These creative activities can even take place during the times you are driving your children to music lessons, school or sporting events. Or presenting a scenario at the dinner table is a great way to generate conversation about the emotions these people are experiencing, and the ways that they might deal with their problems or issues. Once the scenario or story has been told then pose some questions for the children to answer. "How do you think this girl felt when her friends were suddenly so mean to her?" "Has this ever happened to you" What would you do in this situation?" "What advice would you give to this girl if she was your friend?"

Acting out scenarios with puppets is sometimes less threatening for children than telling a story about something that happened to them. Using the puppets helps children to gain some perspective on their own experiences and the ability to examine these experiences without being as emotionally caught up in the events that occurred. Child psychologists and therapists often use play with puppets or other creative materials to explore children's concerns, ideas, and perspectives. Parents can use the same strategies for helping their children develop a strong Emotional Intelligence. Using puppets to act out a play or a dramatic episode also seems less threatening to most children than actually playing a part in the dramatic episode themselves.

Once children are over the age of ten (and of course some younger children as well) they may enjoy engaging in more "adult" activities such as writing or reading poetry to explore feelings. Or using songs and music to explore the emotions they are feeling. The usual or expected flow of information in a child adult relationships are unilateral – that is children seek out information and a sense of direction from adults or parents, and parents "tell" or instruct children. Using Socratic Dialogue in conjunction with these types of creative activities can change this unilateral flow of communications and replace it with dialogue that is more enriching for both parents and children. In using these types of dramatic activities with children be sure to give them the opportunity to present or suggest their own scenarios. You might provide some scripts or stories, but the older children get the more important it is for them to bring the emotional issues to the table that they are concerned about. Parents should be wary of imposing their own agenda – say problem solving about bullying or rejection – because the children or child might want to set a different agenda. Engaging in creative play with children gives them the opportunity to set the agenda and determine which emotions they want to explore.

Chapter 4

How to Foster Emotional Intelligence in Teens

Raising teens is undoubtedly the most challenging stage for parents. Anyone who is a parent of teenagers knows that emotions can be intense at this stage of life. And since teenagers are pulling away from parents and less interested in dialogue, the challenges are many. Children at this stage of development are generally no longer interested in dramatic play with parents or in reading activities with parents. However, literature is still useful for children at this stage of their development and children may be more willing to discuss the characters in a novel and the emotions and choices of the characters rather than discussing their own lives. Parents need to show respect for teenagers' privacy and their right to not reveal information about emotional struggles that may result from peer pressure or conflicts in romantic relationships or with the peer group. When parents are willing to show respect for their children's rights to reveal or not reveal specific details about their lives, they leave the door open to conversation and discussion. Parents may be overly anxious about teenagers and their ability to cope with the complex emotional issues that arise from romantic / sexual explorations and the drama and conflicts that tend to be the norm for teenage peer groups. But parents who show respect for children's privacy are helping their children to develop Emotional Intelligence that will stand them in good stead for this stage of their life and for when they will be moving out on their own. This means that parents should not be Facebook friends with their children, nor should they be monitoring children's text messages or e-mails.

Teenagers go through a similar stage as the "Terrible Twos" in terms of their struggle for independence and their ability to exert self control. Teenagers are as impatient as two year olds since they want to be able to "do for themselves"; however, this time the drive to do for oneself involves more than putting on one's own shirt and pants ! Parents who were patient and supportive of the two and three year olds who were struggling to do for themselves sometimes lose this patience with their teenagers because the stakes are much higher as their children struggle for autonomy at this stage of their development. Parents need to refocus their attention on their own emotions and be self aware about their own feelings as their children become young adults and no longer need so much parental support or protection. Being aware of your own fears and being aware of how to handle those fears appropriately and communicate them to your teenager are important first steps in ensuring that your teens are also developing a high emotional intelligence

Role modeling is, of course, important at all stages of your children's lives. But role modeling is particularly important as your children enter their teen years. They will be quick to spot hypocrisy and the children who once adored you and thought you could do no wrong will now turn into teenagers who are ready to criticize you and point out your faults and shortcomings. Take this shift in the power equation in stride and welcome the opportunity to challenge yourself to change and develop and grow as a parent.

The positive aspect of engaging in Socratic Dialogue with your teens is that their communication skills and their intellectual abilities are developing in leaps and bounds, and you may be pleasantly surprised at the lessons they can teach you. Rather than playing games or even discussing literature it is often best to begin in a straight forward manner with teens and begin to discuss the whole concept of Emotional Intelligence and the best ways for them to foster a strong Emotional Intelligence as they go forward in life. Here are some suggestions for both you and your teen to follow in order to boost EQs. One cardinal rule is to label your feelings rather than labelling the person or the situation. For example, if your teenager is not in by their curfew time and has not contacted you label your **feelings** rather than saying "You are inconsiderate and disobedient when you stay out past your curfew and you are just rude and thoughtless when you do not phone." Instead focus on your feelings in this situation: "I feel very concerned and worried when I do not hear from you when you are not in by your curfew. I worry that you may be in trouble and that you might need help". It is best to use Socratic Dialogues to guide teenagers in the use of these rules. When you forget the rules yourself and lash out and begin labelling behaviours and people, this can be an opportunity to stop and ask "How can I better express my emotions in this situation?"

The second strategy is to help children identify the difference between thoughts and feelings. For example, your teenager might say, "I fell you are unfair when you set my curfew because all my friends can stay out later than me." Use Socratic Dialogue to help you and your child sort out thoughts and judgements from feelings. In this case you can say, "Can you describe to me how you feel in this situation?" The teenager might respond by saying "I feel angry and frustrated when I feel like I might miss out on fun with my friends because I have to come home early". Now use Socratic Dialogue to help your teenagers distinguish between these two statements. Ask them to think about how a parent might respond to both the first statement and the second statement. Hopefully, through Socratic Questioning teenagers will begin to understand that judgemental statements often lead to more confrontation and result in parents becoming defensive about their position and their rules. Teenagers who express feelings as distinguished from judgements might get a more empathetic reaction from parents – or peers, or boyfriends or girlfriends.

A third point to make with your teenagers is the necessity of taking responsibility for their feelings. Point out the difference between saying "You make me angry when you do not come in on time" or "I feel angry when you do not come in one time." Teenagers need to be able to distinguish between what they are feeling and the other person's intentions in eliciting those feelings. Ask your teenager about the difference between these two statements "You are making me feel jealous" and "I feel jealous". The teenager who can claim their own feelings has a better chance of considering why he/she feels a certain way and thinking about whether or not he/she can change the feelings or the situation that is eliciting them.

A fourth strategy is to teach your teenagers how to use their feelings to make empowering decisions. Teach teenagers to ask themselves "How will I feel if I make this choice?" "What can I do to make myself feel better?' Likewise teenagers should learn to ask these questions of others in order to better understand another person's point of view. Role model appropriate behaviours for your teenagers by asking "How do you feel?" "What could you change or do to make yourself feel better?" Your teenagers can learn to draw on their EQs in order to make decisions that will help them to carve out a rewarding and satisfying life. They will also learn to trust their feelings and to listen to their own inner voices in regards to their feelings rather than repressing feelings and taking actions or making choices that contradict their feelings about themselves. Socratic Dialogues can help teenagers gain an insight into how they can use their feelings to set goals for themselves. We often talk about setting goals with our teenagers, but often we do not talk about setting emotional goals. Begin the discussion by posing the question "Do you think people can set emotional goals for themselves? What sort of emotional goals do you think people might set for themselves?" You can also use Socratic Dialogue to focus on a specific goal setting task. For example, you might say "What sort of actions or steps could a person take if their goal was to have a feeling of less anger?" When children are small emotions are generally expressed spontaneously and we often will comfort our smaller children with a hug when they express anger or sorrow. But when our children become teenagers they often mask their emotions and try to hide their angst and even their joy from parents. Being open to exploring your own emotions through Socratic Dialogue and being open to being emotionally expressive yourself are the first steps to encouraging teens to learn appropriate adult strategies for expressing their emotions – particularly anger. Often it is better to keep these discussions on a more abstract rather than a personal level unless your teenager chooses to talk more specifically about his/her own emotional goals. Teach children to use a simple rating scale of 1-10 to evaluate their own emotional responses. Sometimes this is also a good way to engage the entire family in an exercise that will strengthen everyone's EQ. For example if you raise the issue of controlling one's temper and expression of anger. You might ask your teenagers (and of course younger siblings can participate in this exercise as well) to rate themselves on a scale of 1-10 in terms of how satisfied they are with the way they express their anger to others.

It is important to point out to teenagers that anger is not always a negative emotion since this feeling is sometimes an indication of changes or choices that we need to make in our lives. Through Socratic Dialogue teenagers can get some insights into the role that anger plays in our decision making. Pose the question "Can you think of a time when an angry response helped you to make a right choice?" "Do you think that anger can sometimes be a catalyst for change or a wake up call about choices that we are making in our lives?" Through Socratic Dialogue you can also explore the various ways people express anger and deal with their anger. Ask each member of the group or the family what their preferred method is for dealing with anger.

It is also important to teach teens about listening to others without judgement and to reflect feelings back to the person who is expressing them so that they feel that their emotions are validated and recognized. "How do you feel when you are expressing your emotions to someone and they begin to advise, issue commands, or judge the emotions you are expressing?" Teenagers need to learn to recognize that these are invalidating behaviours. It is important to teach your teenagers to avoid relationships with people who invalidate their emotions or people who dismiss their emotions or who respond to their expression of emotions with criticisms or dismissive comments. Remember that the emotional patterns that you set up in your relationship with your teenagers are the emotional patterns that they will be most familiar and comfortable with. Unfortunately, teens can be come "comfortable" with negative patterns as well as positive patterns. If you do not engage your teens in dialogues and show respect for their opinions or points of view, and if you do not validate your teen's feelings and show respect for them when they attempt to express those feelings – then your teenagers will grow into adults who accept relationships in which they are not validated or respected as the norm.

When children are small we can accept that they may be overcome by their emotions and that they may lie down on the floor and weep uncontrollably or throw a temper tantrum. But as children get older we expect them to exercise greater emotional control. One of the best ways to encourage emotional expressiveness in teenagers is to be prepared to engage in conversation about your own strategies and behaviours. Engage in a Socratic Dialogue that invites your children to critique your methods/styles of expressing and dealing with anger. For example, suppose your child does not come in at the agreed upon curfew time, and you become very upset, worried and angry and an angry and heated exchange between you and your child occurs. Once cooler heads are prevailing ask your child some questions about your behaviours: "Do you think my response to the situation was over the top?" "Do you think I kept my emotions under control?" "Can you think of a better way that I might have handled my emotions in this situation?" All too often parents want to engage in a critical appraisal of the teenager's behaviour; however, it is far less threatening to your teenager to engage in a critical appraisal of your behaviour. This type of Socratic Dialogue also gives parents an opportunity to assess their own communication strategies and to view the situation from the perspective of the teenager. When you express your willingness to hear others criticisms and suggestions you are teaching your teenagers an important lesson about being willing to explore the emotional responses of others. These types of exchanges will raise your teenagers EQ and prepare him/her for adult relationships both personal and work related.

It is always less threatening for teenagers to discuss the emotional responses of others – parents, friends, and teachers – than their own emotional responses. And this is the best place to begin when parents are trying to help teenagers develop the skills they will need in order to turn a critical eye upon themselves. By engaging in these types of intellectual exercises, teenagers will develop a vocabulary for discussing and assessing emotions. They will also be able to forgive themselves for their mistakes and to recognize that it is often difficult to engage in "best practices" when emotions are overwhelming logic. When parents share their own stories about dealing with difficult emotions and when they are receptive to listening to their children's criticisms and suggestions, they are setting the groundwork for their children becoming self reflective adults who will be able to respond to the suggestions and criticisms of partners, coworkers and bosses without feeling threatened or attacked.

Often it is best to begin the Socratic Dialogue by focusing on the difficulty of appreciating and understanding another person's perspective and emotional response. Teenagers will often infuriate their parents when they say "There is no reason for you to get so upset" or "You are totally overreacting to the situation". But quite often teenagers are simply reflecting back the comments that their parents have made to them when they have been upset and angry about a situation that their parents deem to be inconsequential or trivial. Parents need to be on guard about making such dismissive comments themselves, and they should point out to their teenagers that it is important for them to acknowledge other people's emotions rather than dismissing them as inappropriate. A good way to initiate a conversation is to ask "If you are extremely upset about a certain situation and someone tells you that you are over reacting, how this reaction makes you feel?" Of course, sometimes a comment about over reacting can be made in a reassuring way, in the sense that a parent or a friend is indicating to the person that they feel like you are worrying too much. However, it is important to teach your teenagers the strategy of always acknowledging the other person's emotional response before suggesting that he/she might not have to be so concerned. Model the behaviour yourself and then have your teenagers role play so that they can practice the strategy of validating others emotions before moving on to solutions or strategies for dealing with a problem or situation.

For example, if your teen is sad and upset because they were not invited to a party or social event do not invalidate the response by commenting "Get over it. The party isn't that important anyway". Engage in Socratic Dialogue to help the teenager explore the emotional response and think about positive ways to deal with his/her upset or unhappiness. Begin by acknowledging and validating the response. "I can see you are feeling upset about the whole situation. Can you tell me some more about it and why you are feeling so sad?" Remember your job as a parent is not to pass judgement on your teenagers, the friends or the situation. Your job is to help your teenagers gain an insight into their own emotional responses and think about how they can resolve the situation and make themselves feel better. Once the teenager has explained why he/she feels badly, then ask "What would make you feel better in this situation? Can you think of anything that you could do that would make you feel better?" These types of dialogues make your children feel like they are in charge of the situation and their feelings and that there are actions they can take and choices they can make in any situation. Sometimes it helps children to gain some emotional distance from a situation if parents say "What advice would you give to a close friend who found herself in this situation?" Sometimes teenagers are better at brainstorming for solution to emotionally charged situations when they cast themselves in the role of the supportive friend rather than in the role of the person needing help. Engaging in this type of dialogue also helps your teenagers to establish a healthy emotional relationship with themselves. Often we do not think about our relationship with ourselves; instead, we focus on our relationships with others. But we all know that we can be our best friend or our own worst enemy. Through the use of Socratic Dialogue you can teach your children to show the same compassion and empathy for themselves that they would show to their friends. Ironically, all of us would often treat a friend better than we would treat ourselves if we were struggling with a problem. And in the same vein we would also be more likely to defend a close friend before we would come to our own defence. By employing Socratic Dialogues parents can help children to develop healthy and positive patterns of "self-talk".

Chapter Five

How Emotional Intelligence Helps Positive Self Talk:

How to Stop the Negative Thinking Reel

Parents should be aware that patterns of negative and positive self talk begin when children are toddlers and during the elementary school years. Parents have the most influence on the "self talk that their children engage in when they are pre-schoolers. Once children attend school they are exposed to teachers and peers who also teach them lessons about self talk. The "self talk" voices inside our heads are the result of tapes that are played over – these tapes consist of comments and responses made by parents as children struggle to learn about how to deal with their emotions and the expression of those emotions. For example, when young children are learning basic tasks such as how to eat with utensils, how to hold a pencil properly, how to write out words or letters, how to tie shoes – they rely on parents for support and encouragement. If parents apply negative labels to children –

you're lazy, you're always so slow to get it, you never try hard enough – these negative comments become internalized and when children get older and are struggling with new areas of competency – unfortunately these negative tapes are often played back in their minds. As parents you need to be asking yourself what knid of self talk you hope your children will engage in as they get older and become teenagers and young adults. We know that people who engage in positive self talk are more resilient, have higher self esteem and feel better about themselves both when they are successful and when they fail. If you are aware that the support and encouragement that you offer to your pre-school aged child and your school aged child will be replayed many times by way of the internal voice, then you are likely to be much more careful about how you respond to your children's efforts to learn and become competent. Some examples of positive comments to make are "go slowly until you get it and then gradually you will get faster"," I admire you when you keep trying and don't give up," "when you try hard I am proud of you and you should be proud of yourself." Now consider how much more powerful these types of statements would be if your children were to self talk in this manner once they were teenagers and adults.

Parents have the most influence on their preschool children, so this is the time to lay the ground work for positive self talk. Children will be exposed to many negative influences once they go out into the world on their own, and we want the positive supportive voices to be the ones that will be loudest in their heads and drown out the negativity that they might be exposed to when other adults or their peer group criticize them or deflate them.

Begin engaging in Socratic Dialogue about positive self talk and the inner voices that speak to us when your children are small. When children are completing an art project ask them to look at each others' pictures and comment on some aspect of the picture that they liked. Then ask the question "How do you feel when someone admires work that you have done?" Children can explore the positive energy that results from being recognized. Then ask the children to look at their own art projects and tell you one thing that they especially liked about their own art project. Explain to children that this type of an activity is self recognition, and that it is just as important as recognizing the good work of others. Now ask the question "How do you feel about your painting or art work now that you have focused on a detail that you really like? Do you feel better about it? Are you feeling like working on the project more and making it better? These types of Socratic Dialogues can help children gain an insight into how empowering self talk can be and how it can inspire them to do a better job and to be proud of their accomplishments.

Also children of all ages are impacted by role modeling. If you beat yourself up and make negative comments about yourself and your efforts, you may not feel that this type of behaviour is consequential. But children mimic the behaviours that they see, and the younger children are the more likely they are to imitate behaviours without thinking about it. These patterns of behaviour then become engrained in their unconscious mind. And negative self talk can become a part of the pattern of how they respond to the world. Listen to the comments that you make about yourself, and also take the time to examine your own internal voices and appraise the kind of self talk that you engage in. Perhaps you have never thought about this before. Often silent behaviours are the ones that go unnoticed and often we are not inspired to analyze them or think about them. It is never too late to change your own patterns of self talk or to inspire your children what ever age they are to change their patterns of self talk to more inspiring and self empowering tapes. Positive self talk increases self respect and resiliency. The person who engages in positive self talk is more likely to solve a problem, think creatively, and not give up in difficult or trying circumstances. If you hear yourself saying things like "I am so stupid. I am so mad at myself for making such a stupid mistake." – Then you are engaging in negative self talk and if you do not identify this to your children they are likely to copy these negative patterns. Seize this teachable moment by stopping and engaging in Socratic Dialogue. "I don't know why I say those things to myself. They only discourage me. Can you think of something better I could have said to myself?" Of course, sometimes our first impulse is to lash out at ourselves through negative self talk. But teaching children to recognize that this is not the most productive response will prepare them for putting the brakes own their own negative self talk.

Socratic Dialogue about the inner voice that your children hear is important at all stages of their development. And even if you follow best practices and ensure that the parent tapes that your children hear when they are young are positive and focused on problem solving and belief in oneself, the world can be a cruel harsh place. Sometimes despite our best efforts our children begin to internalize voices of self doubt and pessimism that are a reflection of teachers, peers, or coaches. Be aware of teachable moments. If you are attending children's sporting events and you hear a coach or fellow team mates berating your child for not performing well enough take the time to explore this situation with your child through a Socratic Dialogue. Sometimes parents may feel that they are teaching their children a lesson simply by pointing out that the coach or team mates were wrong and negative to speak in a disparaging way. But children often still hear the harsh, critical comments inside their own heads and too often repeat these comments to themselves. Instead pose the question "How do you think someone on the team feels when the coach yells at them and criticizes them in front of others?" "Do you think this kind of behaviour is likely to get the person to do a better job or make them feel like they can be successful if they try harder? What do you think the coach could have said that would have helped the person?" These types of questions will start your children on the path to thinking critically about how the comments of others can impact someone. Once they understand the reason for condemning this type of behaviour they are more likely to disregard the negative comments that they hear from peers and coaches and not internalize these comments and make them part of their self talk. Encourage your children to speak up when they hear others making discouraging remarks to others and help them to set personal standards for encouraging both themselves and family members and friends and peers.

One of the simple steps that you can use to teach children positive self talk is get them to choose a mantra. For small children reading a book such as **The Little Engine that Could** is a good place to begin In this case the mantra for the little engine was "I think I can. I think I can." Younger children can enjoy the creative exercise of creating a mantra for themselves, but once children are older they can search for inspirational quotes that they can repeat to themselves in order to reinforce this optimistic mind set and reinforce the habit of positive self talk. Here is one from Winston Churchill that might inspire your children to retain an optimistic attitude and have a more balanced perspective on the trials and tribulations of everyday life: "An optimist sees an opportunity in every calamity; a pessimist sees a calamity in every opportunity". Winston Churchill. Get your children to share inspirational quotes for the day, or share your own inspirational quotes with your children at the dinner table or while driving and then ask them what the quote means to them rather than launching into a parent style lecture on the meaning of the quotation. Here is inspiring advice and a few pithy quotations to discuss with your elementary school children (and your teenagers):

"Live with intention."

"Walk to the edge."

"Listen hard."

"Practice wellness. Play with abandon. Laugh."

"Choose with no regret."

"Appreciate your friends."

"Do what you love. Live as if this is all there is." Mary Anne Radmacher

Listening to quotations and hearing the quotations that their parents or their siblings have chosen to share inspires children to think about their own philosophy and attitude towards life.

Remember that happy, encouraging, positive self talk will boost your child's mental and emotional health. They will have the mental and emotional energy to go forward in life believing in themselves and inspiring others to believe in themselves. The person who engages in positive self talk carries this habit into their interactions with others. And when your children become self aware and better able to recognize and name their own emotions and process those emotions by using a supportive inner voice, they are well on their way to having a stellar EQ. Children who become aware of the inner voice and who have parents who teach them to develop a strong and supportive inner voice are able to claim and deal with all of their emotions – negative as well as positive. One of the most difficult emotions to deal with is anger.

So teaching your children how to recognize when they are angry and how to "self talk" when they experience anger is crucial. Here are some quotations that provide food for thought about anger: "Anger is always more harmful than the insult that caused it." - Chinese Proverb. "Anger is a bad adviser". - French Proverb .When you read these quotations again ask your children what they think the quotations mean and whether or not they can think of an example of when the quotations applied. It is helpful to children if you can recall an incident when the quotation applied to your own behaviour and when you tell a story about a time anger got the better of you and became a "bad adviser". Sharing stories about your own struggles with emotions – particularly anger – gives children permission to admit to their own shortcomings and faults. Turning a critical eye upon yourself and asking your children for their suggestions on how you might have behaved better is more effective than all the parental lectures in the world!

Chapter 6

How Emotional Intelligence Influences Social Relationships and Making Friends

"Walking with a friend in the dark is better than walking alone in the light."

-- Helen Keller

By the time they reach the age of two most children are trying to make social connections with other children. At the age of two, children may simply play next to one another and observe one another. But by the time they reach the age of three children have begun to recognize the patterns of social interaction, and the give and take that is required to play with other children. They need to master the art of taking turns and sharing and of recognizing when other children are upset or angry. Socratic Dialogues can help speed up this process because Socratic Dialogues involve children in the decision making process and the logic of choices. Far too often parents of two year olds assume that they should resolve conflict for children and step in and smooth out the negative aspects of social interaction often without speaking to their children or having a dialogue about why certain choices need to be made or certain actions need to be taken. When you step in and organize the child's experience to eliminate conflict, you are losing the opportunity for a teachable moment. Take for example two children- Paul and Tony- under the age of two. At this stage of development side by side play is more common than truly interactive play. Suppose the two children are playing side by side with different toys. Paul puts down the ball that he is playing with and picks up a block. Tony picks up the discarded ball and Paul then begins to cry and reach out for the ball. A parent might find another ball that is very similar and offer that ball to Paul in order to calm him down. But a better teaching method is to engage in Socratic Dialogue even when children are not necessarily capable of engaging in a conversation. Look directly at Paul and say "Do you want to play ball with Tony?" Often children under the age of two are not capable of engaging in conversation about the social interaction that is taking place. But posing the question sets a pattern of thinking about social interactions. Now look at Paul and say "I think Tony wants to play ball with you. Let's play ball together." By reacting in this manner the parent is helping the child to understand that when we interact with others we can share a toy and play together rather than separately. If parents simply react by trying to pacify each child so that he is happy with the toy he is playing with, then children do not learn the basics of social interaction – taking turns and appreciating another person's point of view. Remember that babies enter the world wired for social interaction, and parents are their first playmates. Even before your child is participating in play with other children the same age, you can begin to teach them the social skills they will need for interacting with others. Babies learn the basics of taking turns, being fair, action and reaction by engaging in play with parents. Parents often forget that the dialogue that accompanies the play is just as important as the play itself. For example, if you sit your eight month old down on the floor and play a game of rolling a ball back and forth use the Socratic Dialogue patterns to help the eight month old develop an understanding of the social interaction. "Who is rolling the ball? Mummy is rolling the ball. Who is rolling the ball? Patsy is rolling the ball? Whose turn is it to roll the ball?

It is Mummy's turn to roll the ball. It is Patsy's turn to roll the ball." Using this patterned dialogue helps children to develop their insights into the roles of social interaction and the principals of turn taking.

Once children are between three and five they develop the language skills and the intellectual skills to think more about their interactions with others and develop more socially. For three to five year olds it is important for parents to talk to them about social interactions. "Who do you like to play with best? Why?" Socratic Dialogues such as these help children to learn about what makes a good friendship and who makes a good playmate or friend. Remember that even negative social interactions are learning opportunities. Children need both positive and negative experiences to be able to understand the complexities of choosing friends and developing friendships. If there is a difficult personality in the playgroup five year olds might be capable of brainstorming about how they can include this person in the playgroup and deal with some of that person's negative behaviours. Three and four year olds, on average, still need help in dealing with children who are overly aggressive or lacking in social skills. Again use Socratic Dialogues to help children gain an insight into these negative social interactions. "Why is it hard to play nicely with Tom? What could you say to Tom that might make him think about what he is doing?" You will be pleasantly surprised at how astute even young children are when it comes to dealing with conflict and other children who do not have appropriate social skills. When social setbacks occur parents can teach their children to develop resiliency and coping skills that will stand them in good stead as they go forward into their school age years.

Parents should also remember the importance of positive role modeling. Children are keen observers and will be watching you attentively when someone is rude to you, or when you might have to deal with an unpleasant or difficult social interaction. If you do not deal well with a negative interaction this is still a teachable moment since you can claim your mistake and ask your children what they might have done in similar circumstances or what they think you could have done that would have worked better.

Children learn best through praise for good social skills and explanations of social protocols and rules for interacting with others. They also learn best by observing your interactions with relatives, your partner, school teachers and other parents. Punishments are less effective than employing praise and natural consequences to teach children about the appropriate rules of social interaction. Whenever your preschool child is behaving inappropriately (being too aggressive, refusing to share, hitting, biting), remove the child from the situation and explain that he/she cannot participate in the play group. The brief deprivation from play will be enough to reinforce to the child that cooperative behaviour is necessary for interaction with other children. The general rule of thumb is one minute of time out for each year of age. While your two year old is having a two minute time out take the opportunity to engage in a Socratic Dialogue. "Why does Davey need a break from playing right now?" If the child is old enough to answer let him provide the reason. If the child is not old enough to respond, then give the answer to the question yourself. Once the child returns to the social situation be sure to praise any appropriate behaviours that you observe so that children learn from both the positive and negative reinforcement. Children need to learn how to pick up on social cues, understand the behaviour of others, and understand the rules of social interaction. By talking to your children and posing questions you invite your children to think about the answers to a problem. At first you may provide the answers to the questions, but children soon develop the ability to respond to the questions you pose. Unfortunately too many parents "do" without talking so that children are not aware of why certain consequences are occurring.

While it is true that some children seem to be naturally more social than others, all children can be taught social skills. Some parents will focus on the nature of their child and simply accept the fact that their child is not as sociable as others and prefers to observe or play alone. It is sometimes hard for parents to draw the line between accepting their children for who they are and not sending messages to the child that his/her personality is unacceptable. Nevertheless, all children do better when they learn about the basics of social interaction. So parents need to be careful that they are not insisting that the quiet or more reserved child be a social butterfly and spend all of his/her time interacting with others or being the center of a social circle. Children who are shier or have more difficulty initiating social interactions need to have more support and encouragement. Many children will display tendencies to withdraw or tendencies not to initiate social interaction with other children even when they are taking part in a play group. In cases like these, parents need to make an extra effort to teach children the basics of connecting with others.

Begin when the child is under the age of two. Make eye contact with your child and give them a big smile. For children who are less social, the emotional responses and the facial expressions or body language may need to be exaggerated. When the baby makes eye contact and smiles be sure to offer praise and respond enthusiastically so that your child is positively reinforced for participating in social interactions. At this point use Socratic Dialogue to teach your children about the flow of information and communication between two people who are socializing. Peek-a-boo is one of the basic social interactive games that parents play with their children (even across several different cultures) since parents seem to instinctively know that this type of game teaches children the basics of making contact with a person and enjoying a playful interaction. Parents automatically engage in a type of Socratic Dialogue when they play this game "Where is Paul gone? I can't see him. There he is Peek-a-boo".

Remember that playing with the preverbal child sets up the basis of knowledge about social interactions. Too many times parents will give their children toys to play with, but they might forget that the best way for children to learn is to engage in play with their parents. The toys are merely props and the parent is the one who uses the toys to teach pre-verbal children the basics of emotional intelligence and social interaction. Once children become verbal and are more interested in playing with peers than parents, then you need to find opportunities for your child to socialize with other children the same age. While parents can find many teachable moments when they play with their young children themselves, parents cannot replicate the authentic responses of same age playmates. Observe your two-five year old as he/she interacts and plays with other children so that you can gain some insight in his/her personality and social style. Take note of areas where your child may need to strengthen his/her social skills and the use role playing at home to help your child learn coping strategies. Sit on the floor with your children and act out scenarios such as fighting over a toy, calling names or asking to play. Then use Socratic Dialogues to help children think about these types of social situations and different strategies for managing them. Remember that giving children solutions is not as effective as having children think about or deduce solutions for themselves. And sometimes you will be surprised by how creative and thoughtful your children can be when dealing with these types of social situations. Play games with your children like Simon Says, Follow the Leader, Duck, Duck, Goose and Tag. This will give you the opportunity to reinforce the idea of following rules, not cheating, taking turns and being a good sport.

When children are between the age of three and five you can engage in some role playing so that children learn how to meet and greet new friends or playmates. Ask your children the question: "What kinds of questions can you ask someone when you first meet them so you can get to know them better? Might you ask the person what their favourite color was? Can you think of any other questions that you might ask?" Also pose questions about what your children might do to engage others. "What would you do if you saw a boy or girl sitting by him or herself in the corner while everyone else was playing?" Posing these types of questions engages your children in thinking about problematic social situations and the type of dialogue is far more instructive than lecturing children about the importance of not excluding others from the play group. Children are much more committed to learning about social interaction when you invite self reflection and give them opportunities to brain storm rather than telling them about the rules and your expectations.

It is also important for parents to help children learn about the types of behaviours that disrupt social interaction and lead to conflict. Sometimes children are not aware of why conflict occurs or why play mates become upset. Talking too loudly, interrupting others, trying to get attention all the time, pulling toys out of the hands of others, name calling, physical aggression – all of these behaviours disrupt social interaction and parents need to actively discourage such behaviours. Children who enter the school system without a basic grasp of the principles of positive social interactions and the strategies for making and keeping friends, often struggle to find a place with in their peer group, and they do not enjoy school as much as children who form friendships with their classmates. We are tempted to issue commands when children are behaving inappropriately "Stop yelling. Be quiet. Don't interrupt". But issuing commands often does not have the desired effect because children have not taken ownership in thinking about their behaviours and whether or not it would be useful to change them. One of the best strategies is to engage in role playing. Tell the child who always interrupts that you are going to do a role play. Have the child tell you a story that he/she knows really well (Red Riding Hood, Three Billy Goats Gruff....) and then keep interrupting them while they are telling the story. Now ask the questions "How did you feel when I kept interrupting you? Could you enjoy telling the story and could I enjoy hearing the story?" Role playing and Socratic Dialogue in tandem give children an experiential grasp of these rules rather than having someone impose the rules upon them without them having a true understanding. Also the focus for children needs to be more on what they should do than what they should not do.

As children become more and more independent and have more opportunities to select friends and make decisions about how they will interact socially with others, their social skills and their social abilities advance in leaps and bounds between the ages of six and nine if they are given the freedom and the opportunity to make their own choices about social activities and friends. Of course, children can only learn through experience, so it is important for parents to give children an opportunity at this age to make mistakes and learn from those mistakes. Far too often parents try to micromanage children's friendship choices and their social interactions at this age. When children are under the age of six, parents are generally responsible for providing opportunities for social interaction and quite often parents are instrumental in choosing both friends and social activities when their children are under the age of six. Many parents are reluctant to let go of this type of control and pass the baton to their children. But it is crucial for children at this age to gain experience in choosing both friends and social activities. Once your children enter the pre-teen, teen years, the consequences of making poor choices in regards to friends and social activities are much more serious than they are when children are still in their middle school years. Children need to gain some experience about choosing friends and choosing social activities wisely (and the two are often closely linked).

During these middle school years children are becoming more aware of the world outside their home, and they are often curious about children (people) whose values and lifestyles are different from their own. During these years children begin to define themselves and gain confidence in their own sense of identity and their own values and beliefs. Although children at this age need some freedom to make their own choices (good or bad), parents still can step in and use Socratic Dialogue to help develop children's critical faculties and their reasoning processes about what makes a good friend. Introduce this topic to your children and ask them "What makes a good friend? What makes you a good friend? Can you think of anyone in your friendship circle who you would say has all the qualities of a good friend?" These types of conversations help children to develop their critical faculties and to recognize that there are certain characteristics that make a good friend. They learn to be more discerning about their choice of friends and they learn to recognize the difference between fair weather friends and friends who have their back during difficult times. It is always tempting for parents to provide the answers for their children and to tell them why they disapprove or approve of certain children as friends. But imposing your judgements on your children is not helping them to develop their own skills in regards to choosing friends who will have a positive impact on the choices they make and their beliefs about themselves.

Of course the person who is a good friend is the person who also tends to have good friends. It is important to discuss with your children the qualities of a good friend and to ask them what they do themselves to be good friends. Between the ages of six and nine children begin to develop preferences for the type of friends they enjoy. This is usually a result of children developing their own interests and personalities. The more opportunities your children have to develop their talents and interests, the stronger sense of self they have. Also the more opportunities they have to discuss their values and beliefs and the more you reinforce your values and beliefs, the stronger will be your child's sense of core values. Children with a strong sense of self and core values will have specific criteria for choosing friends and social activities. This does not mean that your children will not want to experiment with different values or form friendships with children who have quite different values than their own or the values in their family of origin. It is important to allow your children to make the friends that they want to make even if you think these individuals are " troublesome" If you continue to engage in Socratic dialogue methods with your children you will help them discover if this friendship is something they value. Simply telling your children not to hang out with certain individual will not stop them from forming into a certain peer group. The opportunity to test out these values at this age is important since the need to test values at an older age often has more significant consequences and can often lead to more "troublesome behaviours". During the middle school years the consequences might be a school detention, a low grade, a call from an angry neighbour. If children have not had this opportunity then when these values and boundaries are tested during the teen years the consequences can be much more serious.

Discuss potential scenarios with your children since these are less threatening than actually events from their own lives. For example, initiate a Socratic Dialogue by asking "If you were asked to a birthday party but your best friend was deliberately excluded what would you do? How does it feel to be excluded? Have you ever felt left out? What happened? What did you do?" Discussing these imaginary scenarios prepares your child for real life events and helps him/her to think about how they would respond in these situations. Prepare a list of the qualities that make a person a good friend and then ask children what they think about this list. For example, good friends listen to each other and offer empathy and support, good friends do not criticize or call names, good friends will try and help you think of solutions to problems, good friends can disagree with one another without hurt feelings, good friends compliment one another, good friends respect each other and are trustworthy (they do not gossip or repeat confidences), good friends keep promises and are dependable. Parents might provide the list of desirable qualities to children and then ask them if they can think of examples of these types of behaviour either on their own part or on the part of friends. Another strategy if children might feel that this type of exercise is too personal is to have children think about the situation in a more general sense. For example ask children "What sort of names do other children sometimes call others and to why do you think they use name calling?" "What sort of compliments might we give to friends?" When children engage in discussions with their parents about these basic social interactions, they are developing their ability to think critically about social situations and their responses to them.

Parents can also share stories about their own struggles with friends when they were children. This is a good way to engage your children in the discussion of a specific event in a non-threatening manner. It also makes children feel less lonely when they realize that their parents also struggled with the same issues surrounding friendships. If you can share a story about a time you choose an inappropriate friend or a person who later turned out not to be a good friend, you can help your children to realize that choosing and making friends is not an exact science. Also, recalling these stories from your own past can make you a better and more sympathetic parent.

Remember that it takes a lot of experience and exploration before children can learn the basics of choosing and making friends. Give your children enough opportunities to choose friends or playmates and then help them deconstruct the situation if they experience conflict or if a friendship ends. Children learn as much from their mistakes as they do from their successes. Sometimes parents are overly concerned about supervising children when they choose friends and sometimes parents are overly anxious to put an end to friendships that they consider inappropriate or risky. But the important thing is for parents to weigh the benefits of children learning about different personalities and the drawbacks and benefits of choosing certain types of friends. If you feel that your school age children are potentially choosing children who are not "good" or appropriate playmates then take the time to engage in a

Socratic Dialogue with children rather than laying down the law and forbidding them from associating with certain children. As parents, we are often concerned that our children will get into trouble if they make friends with children who are inattentive in school or rude to teachers or cynical and uninvolved in the school community. But it is important to explore through Socratic Dialogue why your child is attracted to this playmate. Begin with a neutral observation "I noticed that you are hanging out with Joey a lot more at recess and after school. Why do you enjoy his company and what sort of games do you like to play together? Does Joey like your other friends and encourage them to join in, or does he want you to play with him exclusively? Why do you think Joey prefers to play with you and does not want to include your other friends?" Ask these types of evaluative questions acts as a catalyst. Your children will be encouraged to think critically about their friendships and their social group and to think about both the dynamics of groups and their reasons for choosing certain types of friends.

Remember not to be excessively judgemental when children are explaining the attraction of a certain friend. If your child tells you that he likes Joey's sense of humour and the way he plays practical jokes on other students or the teacher, do not slip into lecture mode. This is your opportunity to explore the topic of a sense of humour and the morality and ethics of jokes. Children need to reach their own conclusions rather than having these conclusions dictated to them. Sometimes reading an age appropriate novel can help children to gain an insight into inappropriate "jokes" or inappropriate amusements. A good book to read to six to eight year olds is *Owls in the Family* by Farley Mowat. This book features a scene in which the main character Billy comes upon an older boy and his friends who are having some "fun". They have captured some baby owls and put them into an old oil drum and are throwing stones into the oil drum. Billy's solution to this dilemma can provide children for some food for thought. It also provides parents with a non-threatening example of a situation in which children were having "fun" of joking at the expense of the well being of another creature.

Chapter 7

How to Communicate about Bullying and Conflict Resolution

If bullying and teasing is going on in your children's friendship group it is important for parents to intervene and take steps to ensure that appropriate rules are established for social interaction. Most schools these days have educational programs in regards to bullying and teasing and most schools also have a zero tolerance policy for such behaviours. Sometimes parents are unaware that bully and teasing are going on and that either their child or other children in the friendship group are being bullied or teased. Since this type of behaviour is quite common in social groups of elementary school children parents should engage in exploratory Socratic Dialogues with their children periodically to check up on group dynamics. Begin by asking your children questions about the school's policy on bullying and teasing and asking them if their teacher has ever addressed this issue. Use Socratic questioning to inspire brainstorming on the part of children about what type of coping strategies they might use if they ever find themselves in this situation. "What is the best way to deal with bullying or teasing? Can you think of a strategy that might work if you saw a friend who was being bullied or teased by others?" Visual aids sometimes work well and acting out short skits so that children have an opportunity to practice assertive and empowering behavioural strategies in order to deal with bullies.

Children often need help in describing and identifying bullying behaviours. Make a list of the types of behaviours that are engaged in when others are bullied or teased. For example, bullying behaviours would include excluding others, writing notes, gossiping, calling names or making derogatory comments, threatening others physically, making faces. Be sure that children write down the opposite of these behaviours and then think of examples of a situation when they saw both types of behaviour. Positive behaviours that counteract bullying would be including others, complementing others and acknowledging their achievements and contributions, using welcoming and inclusive body language.

Parental role modeling has the most significant impact on children. Parents may unwittingly model bullying behaviours themselves. They may use name calling or exclusion to try and elicit certain behaviours from their children. Shouting at children, hitting them or threatening them with corporal punishment, refusing to show respect for their feelings and opinions, are all examples of parenting behaviours that can be classified as bullying. Remember that if you want your children to develop strong social skills then the best strategy is to model those skills yourself. Of course, parents will lose their cool at some point and may resort to shouting or threats in order to make their children comply with parental demands. When you find yourself in this type of a situation give yourself a brief time out so that you can collect your thoughts and calm yourself down. Then be sure to apologize to your children and explain to them that you have handled the situation inappropriately. When apologizing to children claim the mistake you have made without blame in order to teach your children about the appropriate way to claim a mistake and make amends for a wrong doing. You can also ask your children "What do you think I should have done in this situation? How would you have liked me to handle this situation?" Socratic Dialogues like these encourage your children to think about how to correct mistakes and they learn that you are open to their suggestions.

Sometimes reading a novel or a story about a character who behaves inappropriately or makes a mistake and then apologizes helps children to understand how an apology should be given and received. I recommend *The Wind in the Willows* by Kenneth Grahame.

Sometimes parents will comment that bullying and teasing are just a "normal" part of growing up. And there is evidence that bullying occurs around the globe and cuts across racial and cultural lines and socio economic classes. Just because we see a behaviour being displayed universally, this does not mean that we should chose to normalize or simply accept the behaviour. All children eat with their hands as well and then they learn to use the appropriate utensils and obey the rules of good manner depending upon what culture they participate in. Parents teach their children the rules for good physical health – eating a well balanced diet, getting enough sleep, washing hands before eating. We do not assume that we should just normalize children's desire to eat sweet or rich foods or indulge their desire to stay up late. Likewise, we should be concerned for children emotional well being and recognize that friendships and positive relationships with others are crucial to children's health. Children who are the victims of bullies often suffer from low self esteem if they do not learn how to empower themselves and stand up to bullies. Standing up to bullies need not involve directly confronting a bully – point out to your children that taking action by reporting an incident of bullying or seeking the help of an adult is also a way of being assertive without putting oneself in harms way. Engage in Socratic Dialogue so that children can learn to discern between those situations in which they need to seek the help and support of an adult and those situations which they can deal with themselves. "What can you say when you see another child being bullied? What can you say when another child is bullying you? What should you do if you are being bullied by a group of children?" Role playing or using puppets can help children to gain practical strategies and they will gain more confidence about putting these strategies into effect when they have had a chance to practise them. *Blubber* by Judy Blume is a good example of a book that deals with the issue of bullying. The story is told from the point of view of a fifth grade girl Jill. Jill joins in on the class bullying of an overweight girl in order to win the approval of Wendy. Reading stories like this one gives children an opportunity to comment on the choices the characters make and the consequences of these choices. Read the story to children and then rather than telling the children what the story means ask them questions. "Why did Jill join the rest of the class in bullying Linda? What was Wendy's motive in encouraging others to bully Linda?" Engaging in these types of conversations gives parents an opportunity to enhance their children's thought processes about what makes people "tick". A high social IQ is the result of recognizing others motives and understanding why people seek to influence others or gang up on the one person who is different. Another good novel to inspire discussion about excluding others and being inclusive is Graham McNamee's book *Nothing Wrong with a Three-Legged Dog* and Jerry Spinelli's novel *Crash.*

Teaching Children Skills for Conflict Resolution

One of the most important skills children can acquire during the middle years of elementary school is the skill of resolving conflict with their peers and friends. This skill or talent will stand them in good stead as they go through their teenage years and young adulthood. Conflict is inevitable in social situations and our capacity for resolving conflict and moving forward after disagreements is crucial to determining our happiness and sense of well being in life. Bickering and conflict during childhood years prepares children for conflict resolution as they grow up and the issues and the disputes become more complex with higher stakes attached. The key to conflict resolution lies in the emotional development of children. They must be able to identify their emotions and the emotions of others, and they must have developed a capacity for empathy and the appreciation of another person's point of view before parents can begin to teach some positive strategies for conflict resolution. If your children are still working on expression and control of emotions, then these issues need to be addressed first before parents can begin to develop the skills children will need to discuss a contentious issue and resolve the issue in a way that shows respect for other people's concerns and feelings.

Children learn their first lessons in conflict resolution when they are dealing with parents and siblings, and then they often put these strategies to work in their social/peer relationships outside of the house. Therefore, it is important to use Socratic Dialogues to explore the best strategies for resolving disputes and making decisions when there are disagreements. One of the best strategies is to institute the family meeting. These meetings can happen on a weekly basis. Then if there is a dispute or an issue, children should be encouraged to write it on the agenda for the family meeting. When the dispute or the agreement is ongoing ask "Do you want to add this issue to the agenda for our family meeting? Do you think this would be a good issue to deal with at this week's family meeting? Why is it important for you to bring this issue up at the family meeting?" Remember that asking your children questions like this begins a conversation about the issue and asking these types of questions is an invitation to children to control their emotions and think a bit more about their responses. Children can also prepare for the family meeting by writing down thoughts and concerns and sometimes brainstorming about solutions to the dispute.

 Middle school children can understand the concepts of negotiation, mediation and arbitration. Ask your children about these different terms and then ask them when each strategy is appropriate or useful. Let children know that negotiation with the other people involved in the dispute is the first step to take and that it is preferable if everyone involved gets the opportunity to explain their position and suggest a solution. Point out to children that when they negotiate with others they try to consider their point of view and compromise. For example, a common cause of dispute is sharing a video game or a toy. Parents can ask questions to help children (especially younger children between the ages of 6-8) sort out a fair strategy for sharing a toy or time playing a video game.

Instead of parents arbitrarily imposing a rule about how the video game is to be shared parents should ask the children "Can you think of a fair way to share the game? How can you keep track of who gets to use the game?" Asking these types of questions is a great way to stop the shouting and stop conflicts from escalating. It is important to redirect children's attention to solutions before conflicts become explosive. Sometimes children also become embroiled in conflicts with parents. A good example might be a daily argument over completing homework. Parents are often tempted to create rules "All homework must be done immediately after school. No playing the video game until all homework is completed". When children are not part of the negotiations or the decision making process they have less ownership in abiding by the rules and less ownership in actually achieving the goal. Often they will assert their autonomy in negative ways by trying to circumvent the rules. It is far better to put their creative energies to work by enlisting them in deciding upon a plan or a strategy for achieving the goal of getting homework done on time. Once again, use Socratic Dialogues to broach the issue and make sure the questions are solution focused. "Can you think of a plan or a strategy that you could use to make sure that you complete your homework on time? What are the advantages and disadvantages of doing your homework as soon as you come in from school or finishing homework before dinner? What are the advantages or disadvantages to saving homework until after dinner? Do you think you should always have the same routine, or can you decide on the best time each day?" Posing these types of questions helps children to focus their attention on the underlying goal and they will have more ownership in meeting an expectation if they are part of the decision making process and if they understand why the goal is important.

It is important that children understand that not all conflict between two or more parties can be resolved. And sometimes it is even difficult for parents to resolve a conflict with a child or children. Try as we might sometimes differences or opinions are just too great, or we just can not seem to get ourselves on the same page. Explain the concept of mediation – calling in a neutral third party to help the two people resolve the dispute. Encourage your children to try and resolve their disputes with one another and with friends through negotiation rather than always asking or turning to a parent or an adult for a solution. However, it is important to point out to children that another person who is not emotionally involved in the conflict (whether that person is an adult or in some cases another child) can keep a cooler head and be more rational about looking for solutions. It is important to point out the difference between mediation and "taking sides". Children can use puppets or dramatic skits to learn to distinguish between taking sides and acting as a mediator.

Before the children engage in these dramatic skits teach them about the steps of mediation. The first step is to deal with the angry feelings or the negativity that may have developed between the people involved in the dispute. Again use Socratic Dialogue to help children learn about these three points; "Can we listen to others or focus on solutions when we are feeling angry and upset? Do we feel better when our angry feelings and our upsets are acknowledged by others?" The second step has to do with getting the people involved to commit to the mediation process: "How can you get the people involved to be onside for mediation? How can you get the people to agree to participate in mediation? What might motivate people to participate in mediation?" The third step is to come up with a solution that both parties can agree to: "How can you come up with a solution that both people will be happy with? Is there a way to arrive at a solution that gives everyone at least some of the things that they want?" Asking questions such as these and using Socratic Dialogues teaches children about how to think in a positive way about how to resolve an issue. These questions are pointing the way towards positive problem solving. Far too often parents want to impose a unilateral decision and find the solutions and answers for their children rather than inviting children to find the answers for themselves. Focusing on the behavioural strategy of Socratic Dialogue will ensure that you raise children who have the capacity to think for themselves and come up with positives solution to relationship issues. And it is always important to incorporate education into the Socratic Dialogues – in this case helping children to distinguish between negotiation, arbitration and mediation. Also it is important to ask questions about how much these skills are reflected in the school environment. Many schools have now recognized the value of enhancing children's social development by incorporating opportunities for developing conflict resolution skills into children's repertoire of behaviours. And peer mediation is used in many school environments. If these skills are not being taught in your children's schools, then potentially it is time to advocate for the inclusion of this type of skill building in the school environment.

Chapter 8

How to use the Socratic Dialogue to discuss Sexuality and Romantic Relationships

The ground work for strong relationship skills is established when children are still in their middle school years. During the ages of 6-11 parents tend to spend more time with their children and have more influence over them and more opportunities to talk to them. If children are lucky they enter their teen years with a strong social IQ and they are prepared to navigate the stormy emotions and more complex relationship issues that they will face during their teen years. Unfortunately many parents delay discussing sexuality and romantic or boyfriend/girlfriend relationships until their children are in their teen years. It is far better to discuss these aspects of social development before children reach their teen years. Pre-teens in contemporary society are often involved in romantic relationships between the ages of 11- 13, and many preteens are aware of and curious about sexuality during this stage of their development. Children under the age of eleven are generally less self conscious about discussing these issues with their parents than older children who may feel that such conversations are an invasion of their privacy. Nevertheless, Socratic Dialogues can be used to good effect with all age groups. The most important strategy a parent can remember when dealing with these issues is to avoid becoming personal and try and discuss these issues in the abstract or use examples from popular culture or reality TV shows. Your children will feel much more comfortable dissecting the relationships of these characters and commenting on their choices and their expressions of sexuality than they will be commenting on their own personal lives or the lives of their friends.

Education about sexuality begins even when children are preschoolers. At this age the most important issue is not making children feel uncomfortable with their own bodies or uncomfortable asking questions. When children are very young we often set up a pattern of discomfort in regards to talking about sexuality or sex. We convey to children through our body language or tone of voice that it is embarrassing or taboo or off limits. All children are curious about their bodies and about sex and sexuality. If we become comfortable providing our young children with information about sex and sexuality, we are more likely to feel comfortable talking to them about the more complex issues that arise once they are teenagers such as birth control and the choice of when to become sexually active. Parents often feel discomfort when their young children begin to ask questions about sexuality and sex, and the children will take note of these feelings of discomfort and be reluctant to introduce the subject again.

It is important to work on establishing comfort zones while talking about sex or sexuality. One method for increasing comfort is to use picture books or reading time to introduce the subject of sex and sexuality to children. Since story time is generally a part of young children's routine, this ensures that the discussion and the subject will be raised during a comforting ritual. *"It's Not the Stork"* by Robie. Harris is a great book to introduce preschoolers to the subject of sex and sexuality. Harris has written three books about sexuality for different age groups. The book aimed at preschoolers deals with the basics of how bodies change during adolescence and how parents make babies. There is also some information on appropriate boundaries for touching and private space. Reading one book during story time about this subject is the best strategy rather than choosing to read several books about the theme all at one time. Interpreting these types of picture books with children's favourites and other types of picture books normalizes the topic. When these books are incorporated in this way, discussions of sex and sexuality are less likely to be awkward. Many parents wait for children to broach the subject of sex or sexuality. But children often absorb the message that it is somewhat uncomfortable or awkward for parents to answer these types of questions; therefore, parents should introduce the subject themselves to preschoolers whether or not children ask questions. Do not assume that just because your children have not asked you about sex or sexuality that they are not interested in discussing the topic. *So That's How I was Born* by Robert Brooks is another good example of a book that deals with the subject of sex and sexuality with soft cartoon illustrations.

Providing children with books about puberty and sex when they are between 8-10 is another good strategy for introducing the topic of sex and sexuality without necessarily invading privacy or forcing children to engage in conversation. Robie Harris' book for pre-teens *It's Perfectly Normal: Changing Bodies, Growing Up, Sex and Sexual Health* is a good read for children of this age. Sometimes it is more comfortable to leave the book lying around the house or in the child's bedroom for him/her to find. In this case it is potentially better to give children some space and not raise questions through Socratic Dialogue. While children may want to read the book and think about the information they may feel that dialogues about the book's content are too invasive. Another good book for this age is *A Whole New Approach to Your Body, Brain and Life as a Girl* by Odes, MacDonald and Drill. This book is like having a conversation with another teenage girl who speak to children directly and provides the with some peer advice.

Talking to preschoolers and school age children about sex and sexuality is the best preparation for the teenage years when the questions and answers become much more complex and difficult.

While children may be reluctant to engage in Socratic Dialogue and the specifics of sex and sexuality, it is possible to engage in conversation and Socratic Dialogue about romantic relationships in general. We all want our children to have healthy relationships with peers and friends, but when they embark on romantic relationships and begin to explore intimacy; the possibility for deeper hurts and emotional scars emerges. When your children are still preteens engage in Socratic Dialogue about what the attributes of a positive boyfriend/girlfriend relationship are: "How should a girl/boyfriend treat the other person? What kind of person would you chose for a girl/boyfriend? How do we know when a boyfriend/girlfriend respects us and cares for us? Why do people want to have boyfriends and girlfriends? Do any of the people you know have girlfriends or boyfriends?" These types of generic questions are less threatening and they can speak some interesting discussions and sharing or ideas and values. These types of Socratic Dialogue also give you the opportunity to share some of your values and thoughts or tell stories about your own dating and boyfriend/girlfriend. Sharing your good and bad judgments about girlfriends and boyfriends can give your children perspectives on

106

their own choices and inspire them to be more resilient when relationships fail or their hearts get broken, as they inevitably will.

The best advice is to make sure you lay the ground work for these discussions well before your children are in later adolescence. At this stage, teens are more impacted by peers than they are by parents, and they are less likely to seek out parental opinions or parental guidance. In his case, it is sometimes to focus discussion on celebrities or news stories about sexuality and safe sex. Focusing on the topic as opposed to your teen's choices is less threatening. Once the dialogue has been opened up your teenagers may be more willing to disclose or discuss their own personal circumstances. Sometimes opening the discussion with a Socratic Dialogue about what sort of educational materials or educational sessions are or have been available at their high schools is a good beginning. If you have noticed an interesting news article about teen age sexuality or safe sex practices, ask your teen what he/she thinks of the article. Most teens will not feel as threatened or uneasy if the questions posed are direct and focused on factual information: "Have you had any guest speakers in your school on the subject of safe sex? What is your sex education class like? Do you think that sex education classes should be held separately for males and females? Should co-ed classes be the norm?" These types of questions lay the ground work for opening up conversations about sexuality with your teenagers. And you may get some interesting perspectives on the sex education that is being offered to your teens. It is also a good idea to invite your teenagers to criticize the sex education programs at their schools and ask them what sort of information they would provide and how they would convey that information if they were in charge of the sex education program. These types of Socratic Dialogue will give your teens an opportunity to explore their attitudes towards this topic in a non-threatening way since the questions are not personal or invasive. Avoid initiating dialogues that focus on your teens' behaviours. Do not ask "Have you had sex? Do you know how to practice safe sex?" While such blunt questioning may seem important and responsible to parents, this type of questioning and invasion of personal space will quickly shut down communications between parents and teens. Let you teens decide how much personal information they want to share about their sexual experience or sexual knowledge. This is one of the steps towards adulthood – recognizing that sexual matters are often not an appropriate topic of conversation. After all, as a parent you do not expect to have your teen question you about your sexual behaviours, and since your teens are en-route to becoming adults, you need to accord them the same respect and the same boundaries that you would establish with any other adult.

At this age teens want to test out their sexual attractiveness and explore their values in regards to intimacy and respectful and enjoyable relationships. It is sometimes best for parents to focus on the non-sexual aspects of a relationship so that teens will recognize that sex is only one element of a satisfying relationship. When parents become over concerned about whether or not their teens are engaging in sex, they often attempt to establish rules of conduct that will prevent teens engaging in any sort of sexual exploration. This type of controlling behaviour is only likely to cause teens to be deceptive with parents and to resist talking about sex or safe sex with parents at all. Far better for parents to focus teens' attention on the non-sexual side of relationships since this is an aspect of relationships that is often overlooked or underestimated by teens when teen culture focuses on sexual activity. Teens who talk about relationships and what intimacy and respect in a relationship means are more likely to make wiser choices about when to become sexual active. Remember that teens between the ages of 15-19 need lots of opportunities to hang out with friends and interact with a wide range of personalities. They are testing the waters and trying to determine why they are attracted to others and what aspects of a relationship are important to them. Encourage teens to socialize with large groups of friends and try and provide opportunities for them to meet teens from outside of their neighbourhood or peer group. Remember the more your teens know about relationships and sex, the healthier and more empowering their relationships will be.

It is important to ask your teens why they might want to encage in sex. Once again a warning about addressing the question in a personal and specific way that shows no respect for your teens' privacy. Ask the questions from the third person perspective. "Why do you think teenagers decide to have sex? Do they always actively decide? Do you think people should have casual sex if they are not involved in a committed relationship? What do you think your friend's definition of a committed relationship would be? Is their definition of a committed relationship the same as your? Do you think that most people use birth control when they have sex? What else might people have to worry about besides an unplanned pregnancy if they decide to have sex?" it is important to ensure that teens at this age do have the right information about sexually transmitted disease and the potential for an unplanned pregnancy. Be sure to ask some general questions about birth control and the effectiveness of birth control. "Do you know of anyone who has gotten pregnant when taking a birth control pill? Do you know why this happened?" Quite often teens who are taking birth control will forget that if they have to take an antibiotic or if they are ill and they are sick to their stomach, they may compromise the effectiveness of the birth control pill. It is also very important for teens to realize the difference between protecting themselves from sexually transmitted diseases and protecting themselves from an unplanned pregnancy. Again, instead of discussing the situation from a personal perspective or lecturing your children about the dangers of sexually transmitted disease, use Socratic Dialogues to encourage teens to come to the right conclusions by themselves. "Do you think that sometimes people worry so much about birth control that they forget to think about the danger of sexually transmitted disease? Do you know anyone or someone who trusted a partner and then found out that they caught a sexually transmitted disease from that person?" Often it works well to discuss cases from popular culture. Television series like *Degrassi the Next Generation* often address such issues as sexuality, teen pregnancy, and peer pressure.

Most parents feel that these discussions are somewhat awkward. However, most of the awkwardness is the result of making discussions too personal. Those feelings of awkwardness or discomfort should be respected. Take a step back if you feel that there is awkwardness or discomfort and find ways to introduce the subject in a way that is non-threatening. If you feel uncomfortable giving your teens specific information about birth control or specific information about sexual safety, there are plenty of reading materials that you can provide to ensure that your children have the time and opportunity to absorb the information in a non-threatening atmosphere. It is your responsibility as a parent to ensure that your teens have adequate knowledge of sexuality and safe sex practices. Providing them with accurate information is not providing them with a license to become sexually active. In fact, the research shows that teens who have the most information and a good understanding of some of the negative consequences of engaging in sexual relationships are more likely to delay sexual activity. It is somewhat ironic that parents will often assume that if teens have knowledge about sex and about birth control and access to birth control that they are more likely to become sexually active. Remember that when teens are well informed they can make better choices and they can feel empowered to protect themselves and to resist peer pressures to engage in sexual explorations that they are not comfortable with. According to a survey commissioned by NBC News and *People Magazine,* 87% of 13- to 16-year-olds report having never had sexual intercourse, and 73% report having not been sexually intimate at all. It is important to share these facts with your teenagers who may feel that the majority of their friends have already been sexually active.

Remember that your role as a parent is to provide information and to let your teens know that you are available for discussion or questions if they have any. However, there is always a certain awkwardness in terms of parents and children sharing specific details or personal information, and personal boundaries should be respected. Instead, encourage teens to talk about the subjects of the choice to become sexual active, birth control, safe sex and protection from sexually transmitted disease from a more abstract perspective. Sharing news stories or commenting on people in TV shows or in the popular press is preferable to trying to delve into the specifics of your teenager's private life

Chapter 9

How to Use Emotional Intelligence to Increase Cognitive and Intellectual Abilities

I have saved the fourth dimension for the last since this is the dimension that is most focused on by the education system. Often parents will leave intellectual development to the schools and will simply read report cards and consult with schools about their children's intellectual development. Parents may see themselves as only performing a supportive role when it comes to children's intellectual development. However, parents are crucial to this process because it is often the parents who influence children's attitudes towards intellectual curiosity. Parents need to stimulate their children to be intellectually curious so that they can begin to learn for themselves. Only the truly intellectually curious will process information and take ownership of knowledge because they want to understand. Many children got through the motions of seeking an education, but they are not truly intellectually curious. Parents of preschool children may unwittingly discourage intellectual curiosity in young children by using phrases such as "You ask too many questions. You are too young to understand. I will explain that when you are older." The strength of establishing patterns of Socratic Dialogue in all areas of your family life is that the encouragement is there constantly for children to realize that life is a process of forming questions and seeking answers. When parents pose questions for children and help them find the answers they are teaching their children that part of the process of intellectual growth is formulating questions and discovering answers. While it can be frustrating to try and answer children's questions and while it may at times be easier to discourage rather than encourage their inquisitiveness, your efforts will be well rewarded when you raise children with strong intellects and higher IQ's.

Remember that cognitive development and intellectual curiosity are different than simply memorizing facts or chanting the letters of the alphabet. Cognitive development has to do with encouraging children to use their reasoning processes and their logic and challenging them to come up with solutions. Cognitive development usually goes hand in hand with language development. So when you are speaking to children under the age of three the more you include some analysis and logic in that talk the more your child will display these logic skills when he/she begins to talk. Incorporate the five w's into your talk with your children ("Who, what, why, where when). By the time the child is beginning to speak more at the age of four or five you will be surprised at how these skills are now reflected in their speech and the way they talk.

Verbal games are great to use when children are young. You have a captive audience and they still love to play with parents and caregivers. This is an ideal time to stimulate their intellectual curiosity and their ability to solve problems by playing verbal games with them. Children (even babies) love puzzles and the surprise of discovery; hence the popularity of the game of peek-a-boo with infants under the age of eight months. Far too often parents are using electronic entertainment to pacify children rather than actively engaging them to stimulate their intellectual growth. Most of these verbal games are based on the Socratic Method of posing a question and asking children to figure out the solution. "I spy" is a tried and true version of a logic game. "I spy something brown that is shaped like a box, but it is not a box". These traditional games are, unfortunately dying out as parents decide to hand their smart phone to the young child in order to pacify him/her by allowing them to push buttons that provide them with a momentary change in stimulus (usually visual or auditory). Another verbal game to play is a simple recall game "What did you wear yesterday? What did you eat for breakfast this morning? What color is Daddy's coat?" These types of games are challenging children's cognitive abilities – their ability to recall and to recognize the cues that they have been given in order to get the "right" answer. Another basic logic game to play is to make a statement that children can respond to with a simple "yes" or "no". For example, "Chickens can fly. Elephants can fly". These types of games will stimulate children's ability to think about problems and puzzles and find solutions. Since few props or toys are needed for these types of games, parents should always remember the basic format of these logic games for young children when they find themselves stuck in traffic or stuck in a line. Playing these engaging games makes the time go by quickly; parents are seizing a teachable moment and they are amusing and engaging their children when they might otherwise be bored or restless. Another game to play is one that challenges children to recognize different categories. You provide a list and they determine what does not fit in the list. For example, consider the following list: "Shoe, shirt, pants, and homework". Children enjoy this type of logic game and they can of course put their logic to work by inventing a list for you.

With slightly older preschool children parents can also play the "What if?" game. "What if all the power in the house went off what would we do? What would you do if you got lost in the store and could not find your parents? What do we do when it snows?" The questions posed can be adjusted to match the intellectual abilities of your children. The "What if" game can also prepare children for empowering decision making when they find themselves in trouble. "What should you do if a stranger asks you for a ride home? What should you do if you feel uncomfortable with a request from an adult?" Asking the "what if" questions prepares your children to think logically and analytically about different situations. We cannot always be there to protect our children so we should remember the adage "forewarned is forearmed". Playing this type of game enables your children to think about various problem solving strategies for problems that they might encounter. Of course these problems can be of the more mundane version as well. "What would you do if you forgot your lunch at home and you were hungry? What would you say to the teacher if you forgot to do your homework? What would you say to another child in your class if they asked you for some of your lunch?" Even young children encounter problems and difficulties in the course of their daily lives. The more prepared they are to think both creatively and logically about solutions to problems the more resilient they will be and the better they will be able to weather the daily trials and tribulations of life.

Some children are very active and restless, but parents can still stimulate their cognitive abilities by making physical movement part of the intellectual game they are playing. For example parents can play the traditional game of hotter/colder. Children move around the room and the person indicates whether they are "hot" or "cold" depending on how close they are to the chosen object. This can be combined with providing clues or getting the children to ask questions that focus on clues. Other traditional games that stimulate cognitive growth are "Hide and Seek", Charades, or Twenty Questions. Parents need to remember these traditional methods for engaging in questions and discursions with their children. These types of games encourage interaction between parents and children and encourage teachable moments. Unfortunately with all the technology that parents have access to today, children are less and less likely to play these types of traditional games that are so well suited to stimulating cognitive development and children's operative IQ. These games are active while video games and media entertainments are often passive so that children are not fully engaged in problem solving and actively involved in thinking and using their logic skills. Often children are simply mesmerized by a quickly changing stream of visual and auditory stimuli. However, the electronic versions of some of the traditional games that stimulated children's intellectual growth are useful, because often the child does not need to have an opponent. Some examples include snakes and ladders, battleship, tic tack toe, and dominoes. Remember that your children's games are serious business. When they are playing you want them to be actively involved in the game so that they are developing their cognitive abilities and their ability to examine problems from different angles and think creatively about less apparent solutions. Building toys offer the same opportunity for children to develop their logic, their special sense and their planning skills and strategies. Parents often mistake the idea of learning facts and being able to recite or regurgitate material as a sign of intellectual strength. In reality, children who are above average thinkers and above average problem solvers will have the edge when it comes to higher IQ's. And the best part is that old fashioned game playing versus expensive lessons and/or toys is the best way to accomplish the goal of strengthening your preschooler's IQ.

Another cautionary note to add is to allow your preschooler to use imagination freely. Another common mistake that parents make with preschoolers is their belief that children who understand the difference between make believe and reality are more advanced cognitively and intellectually. Not so. Children under the age of five use imagination and make belief to stimulate their intellectual growth and their capacity for problem solving. Children's capacity to come up with imaginary "out of the box" solutions to problems or dilemmas at this age is a sign of intellectual and cognitive strength. Parents who insist that children give up their make believe friends or their belief in fairies, Santa Clause, and the Easter Bunny are failing to recognize that all children go through a stage of development when the lines between reality and fantasy are blurred. And it is important to honour this stage of development and their capacity for blending the real with the imaginary. Children who have been given the opportunity to strengthen their imaginations through creative and make belief play have much stronger IQ's when they become preteens, teens and young adults. They are able to think about problems and issues in many different ways, and they are better able to turn a problem around and examine it from several different angles, and better able to appreciate a variety of different opinions and solutions without automatically dismissing those solutions that one first glance may seem unworkable.

Sometimes adults and parents have difficulty entering children's imaginary worlds or engaging them in discussions when they blur the boundaries between reality and fantasy. This is why the principles of Socratic Dialogue are so useful. Instead of insisting that your preschoolers join you in your world, enter their world and explore that world by posing questions and listening to their responses. "What is the name of your imaginary friend? Where does he or she live? Why do you suppose I cannot see this friend? Which world is better – your imaginary world or this world? Why?" Generally children three and under have greater difficulty in differentiating between the real and the imaginary; therefore, they are often afraid of the monsters that come out after dark. Children over the age of three can distinguish between reality and fantasy, but the boundaries between the real and the fantastical are very fluid, and they do not always see that there is a pressing concern for distinguishing between the two. At this stage children are still actively involved in constructing the appropriate boundaries between the pretend and the real. Therefore, it is appropriate at this age to engage in Socratic Dialogues that help children with this stage of cognitive development. "Can you really fly, or do you like to pretend that you can fly when you play your game? When you are pretending do you almost convince your self that you can fly?" Reading books that explore the boundary between the real and the fantastical is always helpful. One favourite with parents and children is Maurice Sendak's *Where the Wild Things Are.* You can also play the "Yes/No" game to help children distinguish between the real and the fantastical. Get children to answer yes or no. "There are monsters that come out from under our bed at night time. Sometimes we imagine there are monsters under our bed at night time." Reading the classic fairy tale and folk tales and reading or chanting nursery rhymes also helps strengthen children's cognitive abilities. They begin to develop logic skills and the ability to judge what is real or not real. At this sage in children's lives it is very important to monitor the type of television programs that they are watching. Because children do not have the ability to distinguish between reality and fiction, they can be overwhelmed by some of the more graphic content on TV. Be sure to monitor the TV watching of your preschoolers since excessive TV watching can impair cognitive growth because it is such a passive activity that does not activate children's critical reasoning skills. As much as possible, watch TV with your children and again use a pattern of Socratic Dialogue to activate their critical sensibilities when they are watching TV. This type of dialogue is particularly important so that children can distinguish between advertisements and TV programs and recognize when they are being "sold" a product. Even very young children are able to dissect the psychology behind certain TV advertisements. "Is this an advertisement or a TV show? Is the advertisement trying to convince you that you should buy the cereal or the toy? How do they try to convince you?"

Piaget referred to the stage of development that take place between the ages of seven and eleven as the concrete stage of cognitive development. Children at this stage have a firm grasp of the boundary between reality and make believe even though they still enjoy games of make believe and dressing up and acting out different parts and roles. However, at this stage children still struggle with abstract thought processes and they are still in the process of learning basic facts and concepts about how both the physical and the social world work. As they go through this stage of development children come to better understand the concepts of cause/effect, comparison/contrast, classification and categorization. Parents will often feel that they should give their children extra homework or classes at this stage of their lives to prepare them for success in high school. It is far better to play games with children that will increase their awareness of these logical patterns of reasoning.

Many parents feel like the IQ of teenagers has taken a step back rather than a step forward. This is often the result of the fact that social and emotional growth are at the forefront of the development at this point in time. Teens are highly distractible and their frontal lobes that deal with logic, reasoning and information processing are still growing. There are greater expectations that teens will be able to discipline themselves and memorize and integrate academic materials so that they can achieve the grades that are necessary for pursuing career goals. Parents, once again, often focus on homework completion, hiring tutors, letter grades achieved in school, and competitiveness with peers in terms of academic performance. While it is understandable that parents are concerned that their teens will be successful in school and earn the academic credentials that will give them more choice in terms of the types of careers they can pursue as adults – it may be comforting to know that a dismal academic performance in high school does not always correlate with a low IQ. Often teens are simply disinterested in academic studies at this point in their lives because they are focused on their social group and peer relationships- romantic or otherwise. Teens have so many other issues to deal with that the time and energy that they might spend on academic pursuits is directed towards making choices about values, adult identity, choices about sexuality, and choices about values. Tests carried out in 1980 and again in 2008 show that the IQ score of an average 14-year-old dropped by more than two points over the period. Among those in the upper half of the intelligence scale, a group that is typically dominated by children from middle class families, performance was even worse, with an average IQ score six points below what it was 28 years ago. The problem is that more and more teens are being entertained and engaged in media. They read less and they have fewer conversations of a complex nature with both peers and parents. This information provides us with some clues of the steps we parents can take to promote cognitive abilities during the teen years. Discussions with parents become even more significant as the teen brain continues to develop and the adult intelligence and personality begin to become more stable. Parents need to recall the same patterns that they focused on during the middle school years in their conversations with their children – causes and effects, comparisons and contrasts, definition of terms, and classification and categorization. Take every opportunity you can to engage your teens in conversations about whatever issues they are interested in , but be sure to focus discussions on these patterns in order to strengthen teen's logical abilities and their ability to draw reasoned conclusions about any issue or problem. Spend less time harassing your teens about the number of hours of homework that they are doing or hiring tutors to improve their grades. Spend more time asking them questions and exploring their logic and reasoning processes on a wide variety of topics. It is often best to chose topics that are near and dear to your teen if you do not want the Socratic Dialogue to end, and if you hope that the dialogue will be lively and thought provoking. Many of the questions raised for discussion can be the same as the questions posed for contemplation of your preteen children. "Who is the most popular person in your peer group? Why do you think this person is popular? Do you think it is important to be popular? Would you like to be more popular?"

Avoid judgemental responses to your children's responses. Do not come to the dialogue prepared to lecture them on the superficiality of the standards for popularity in high school. Instead, be prepared to explore the whole abstract concept of popularity or status and what this entails in a non-judgemental ways. It is wrong to be dismissive of your teens concerned or of the standards for stouts and popularity that are often established by a peer group. Remember the idea is not to lay down the law or provide definitive answers. The goal is for your teenagers to explore a subject through conversation. Ask questions that invite teens to look towards the future since they tend to be very "in the moment" thinkers. For example, ask your teenager "Do you think the criteria for social status or popularity changes once a person graduates from high school? What are some of the differences and similarities between the way status is determined in high school and the way status might be determined in the workplace or on a college campus?"

One important aspect of stimulating cognitive growth and this stage of life is helping teens to bridge the generation gap, and developing their ability to appreciate the perspectives of different people on different topics or issues. When children are younger, they expect definitive answers. They have less ability to understand that there are sometimes several answers to the same questions, and that sometimes these answers may sometimes even appear to contradict each other. People with higher IQ's have the capacity to think in a multidimensional way, so try and engage in activities and dialogues that stimulate your teens to appreciate the multidimensional perspectives on problem solving. Often it is hard to bridge the gap because teenagers perceive parents as "the enemy"- someone who is trying to restrict or control their actions and choices. One way to bridge the generational gap is to engage in negotiations with your teens rather than laying down the law and demanding conformity to certain rules or standards. Take time to discuss the issue with your teenager. For example, if you have a curfew, be sure that you sit down with your teens and negotiate the time of the curfew and each of you should have the opportunity to present your point of view and your ideal "boundary". Try and use Socratic Dialogues to arrive at a compromise that both parents and teens can commit to. "What time do you think your curfew should be? Why is a curfew necessary? What kind of protection does this offer to the person who commits to the curfew? Do you think it is acceptable for teens not to have a curfew at all? How do parents feel when teens do not make their curfew? What actions should your teen take if he/she is not going to be able to make the curfew?" You can even choose to sign a contract with your teen that spells out the conditions of the curfew. Sometimes drawing up a document and going through the process of having both parents and teens sign the document is an experience that can bridge the generation gap. In this case, there can be no dispute about what the agreement was on the part of both parties. Penalties and consequences of violating the contract can also be decided upon in advance so that teens developing their cognitive abilities to think about the consequences of actions – whether positive or negative. And parents should try to remember the importance of positive reinforcement as well. Too often parents will focus on the negative consequences that will occur if teens to do abide by the rules. But they do not offer rewards to teens who remember the rules and make a commitment to them.

When children are older, the stakes are much higher and it is tempting to let the lecturing begin and make every effort you can as a parent to stop teens from making mistakes. Active listening becomes even more important at this stage of your children's development. This can sometimes be difficult since teens will often consciously or subconsciously choose an inconvenient moment to share information, or ask for permission, or make a request that they feel you might deny. If it is not possible to stop what you are doing and make eye contact with your teen and give them your undivided attention, then indicate to them when they can have your undivided attention so that they can explain the situation, problem or request to you. Active listening means that you repeat back to your teen both the information that he/she has conveyed and your interpretation of the emotion as well. Once you have summarized the information and the feeling then check in to ensure that you have interpreted them correctly: "I hear that you are concerned about your math grade and you feel frustrated because you can not get enough help from the teacher, and you are worried that you might fail the course and have to repeat it. Is that correct?" When you restate the teen's concern they feel like you have heard the problem and that you understand why they are upset. Give your teens time to brainstorm for their own solutions, or ask them what solutions they can come up with rather than offering to rescue them or imposing a solution on them. You can brainstorm with them and provide some suggestions yourself, but you need to ensure that the brainstorming session is a collaborative one. Active listening skills means that parents employ questions that open the door to further conversation rather than shutting down the conversation,. Any judgemental phrases or pronouncements are going to end the conversation; "Failure is not acceptable. We will hire a tutor and then you will pass the course. You're just not trying hard enough." Instead parents need to ask open ended questions that will enhance their teens IQ – or their cognitive abilities. "Do you know anyone else who is in the same situation? Can you think of any solutions to the problem? Are you too upset to think about solutions right now? I can understand why this is worrying you. Do you want to tell me more?"

Making sure your teens are active agents in planning their lives and resolving their problems will enhance their cognitive abilities as they enter adulthood. Too often parents are not focused enough on the generic skills of being able to think, plan , set goals , and decide on how these goals can be accomplished. Parents may be more focused on setting goals for their children and then micromanaging the circumstances in their lives to ensure that they have optimal conditions to achieve those goals. Unfortunately, this type of parenting does not prepare teens for the challenges of young adulthood when they head off to college and university and into the workforce where parents can no longer control their environment and intervene on their behalf.

Making a Commitment to the Socratic Method

Making a commitment to the Socratic Method of interaction and dialogue with children from a very young age can enhance growth in all three dimensions of their lives – the emotional, social, and intellectual. If you have not employed the Socratic Method with young children, you can begin to use this style of interaction to improve your communications with your children no matter what age they are. Establishing a dialogue with children ensures that they will feel acknowledged and heard. Soon this pattern of communication becomes second nature and begins to be an entrenched part of family culture. Hopefully the examples and tips in this book have focused your attention on establishing conversations with your children rather directing and lecturing. One of the challenges of modern family life is too make time to listen to one another and engage in conversations. Family mealtimes or bedtime rituals provide perfect opportunities to spend some time in conversation with children and family members. But there are also brief minutes during the day when you can take a few moments to ask your children questions and then really listen to what they are saying by giving them your full attention. As parents we often think that our role is to provide our children with answers, but children learn much more when they discover the answers for themselves. So listen to yourself the next time you are interacting with your children and take note of how many times you ask your children a question and then give them your full attention and encourage them to think about their answer.

Printed in Great Britain
by Amazon.co.uk, Ltd.,
Marston Gate.